TAROT
RITUALS

About the Author

Nancy Antenucci (Nucc) is a full time reader, teacher, and storyteller. Nucc's first career was that of a dancer and choreographer. She is based in Minnesota and has created a strong community of tarot lovers. She helped build and is a faculty member for a tarot school in China. She believes that David Bowie is one of her divine allies. She can be reached at www.betweenworlds.us.

NANCY C. ANTENUCCI

Ceremonies, Ideas
& Experiences for
the Tarot Lover

TAROT
RITUALS

Llewellyn Publications
Woodbury, Minnesota

FIRST EDITION
First Printing, 2022

Book design by Samantha Peterson
Cover design by Shira Atakpu
Tarot spreads by Llewellyn Art Department

Llewellyn Publications is a registered trademark of Llewellyn Worldwide Ltd.

Library of Congress Cataloging-in-Publication Data
Names: Antenucci, Nancy, author.
Title: Tarot rituals : ceremonies, ideas & experiences for the tarot lover
  / Nancy C. Antenucci.
Description: First edition. | Woodbury, Minnesota : Llewellyn Publications,
  2022. | Summary: "Merges tarot reading for the self/others with
  spiritual ritual (individual or group)"— Provided by publisher.
Identifiers: LCCN 2021043622 (print) | LCCN 2021043623 (ebook) | ISBN
  9780738764443 | ISBN 9780738764740 (ebook)
Subjects: LCSH: Tarot. | Rites and ceremonies.
Classification: LCC BF1879.T2 A565 2021 (print) | LCC BF1879.T2 (ebook) |
  DDC 133.3/2424—dc23
LC record available at https://lccn.loc.gov/2021043622
LC ebook record available at https://lccn.loc.gov/2021043623

Llewellyn Worldwide Ltd. does not participate in, endorse, or have any authority or responsibility concerning private business transactions between our authors and the public.
  All mail addressed to the author is forwarded but the publisher cannot, unless specifically instructed by the author, give out an address or phone number.
  Any internet references contained in this work are current at publication time, but the publisher cannot guarantee that a specific location will continue to be maintained. Please refer to the publisher's website for links to authors' websites and other sources.

Llewellyn Publications
A Division of Llewellyn Worldwide Ltd.
2143 Wooddale Drive
Woodbury, MN 55125-2989
www.llewellyn.com

Printed in the United States of America

*This book is dedicated to the innocent one whose
heart is a wren, dancing Hierophants, and to my mother,
Evalyn and her line of mothers—may I reflect all of you in Love.*

CONTENTS

CONTENTS

RITUALS, SPREADS & TEMPLATES

Chapter Four

Chapter Five

An invitation to engage with one or a group of Divine Allies from other realms.

Asking for messages from your body, intellect, emotional self, your spirit, and guide as an introspective practice.

Focusing on each of the seven chakras for an energetic overview.

Examining the deeper message of a dream utilizing your natural associations and cards.

Three ways to explore your light self, the shadow self, and the dark self.

Chapter Eight

Chapter Nine

Chapter Ten

ACKNOWLEDGMENTS

My greatest gratitude goes to Tim Breslin, who edited and researched diligently so I sound smart; the Schmidt family for allowing me time at the holy farm to have the support of trees as I write; Sam Lofgren, who compassionately challenged any nonsense; Rita Chakrabarti, who is not only the perfect reader for this book but made it a way better one as well; Tanya Brody for her warm insights; Barbara Moore, my dear Babs, for encouraging me to write another book from my heart; and my guys, Chris and Alex, for their daily support and love.

FOREWORD

I am honoured to greet you at this frontier where life-by-default rubs elbows with life-by-conscious-choice, where rational knowing and other-than-rational knowing may lock eyes and talk, and where you and I meet at last yet somehow again. Let's cross this threshold and companion one another through Nancy Antenucci's *Tarot Rituals*, cards in hand.

More than words on pages, the book you've now entered is rich territory where the author has set up a spiral path for you. Be prepared to encounter structure and fluidity, practical techniques and theoretical leaps of faith, tried-and-true information, terrifying explorations of imagination, a strong *no* to bullshit, and a strong *yes* to your truth. This symbol-festooned journey will delight you, unnerve you, illuminate your brilliance, piss on your parade, and do whatever the Part of You That Knows You Best needs to do in order for you to remember and become more of who you really are, then allow that to ripple into our world in a good way. If at any point this feels daunting, employ the tarot as your anchor, map, and creative springboard—touch the pasteboards, observe the symbols, reflect on the concepts, apply the insights, and carry out your self-generated ceremonies.

If you aim to use *Tarot Rituals* to sharpen (or discover!) your skills as a tarot consultant and provide more personal, informative, and useful readings, you'll be sumptuously rewarded. Nancy's simple, effective methods to open, maintain, and close a tarot session will incontrovertibly signal to your wisdomsource(s) when you're turning it to tune in, when you need the flow of conversation with soul and spirit to remain loud and clear, and when you're turning it off to tune out and get on with life. Make a ritual of these practices to make your readings shine!

If your Core Self thrums with 13.8 billion years of power, love, creativity, and wisdom carried all the way from the moment of the Primordial Flaring Forth ("Big Bang") to the breath you're currently taking, you'll find affirmation herein. If your soul understands at the deepest ritual level that to dance for the healing of your skin and blood *and* for the soil and water of our planet with tarot characters such as Strength and the World, to sing for political change while entranced by the powers of Justice and the Tower, to moisten your silky Hierophant drag with sex juice as you make messy, vociferous love with the Devil to curb humanity's self-destructive tendencies, you will find encouragement. As a Magician of the Feminine, Nancy's magick is *embodied*. The days of armchair magicians verbally wanking at each other are over. Dire circumstances and unsettling times require ceremonies that blaze with unprecedented originality so we can enflesh what is sacred to us, flick the first domino of the collapse of an unhealthy status quo, to be, in the words of poet June Jordan, the ones we have been waiting for.

I'm writing this foreword in September of 2020, a month which marks 41 years since the tarot came into my life and 25 years since it became a tool I use on a professional basis to coach, counsel, and teach clients and students. For 13.5 of those years, Nancy Antenucci has been a true friend, a soul sister, and an astonishing tarot colleague. We met at a tarot conference in April 2007. Ever since that epiphany of connection, she and I have laughed at one another's dirty jokes, cried for one another's losses, supported one another's private practices, raged with one another over unjust policies, savoured witty banter and important news via video chat and over in-person meals, and provided "aha" moments for one another with and about the cards. The privilege of witnessing Nancy's skill as a tarot professional and her fierce love for all that is truly good have inspired me to trust her. So can *you* as you take a seat in our council of symbols and friends here in *Tarot Rituals*.

by James Wells
https://jameswells.wordpress.com

xxv   Preface

PREFACE

Welcome. I created this book for those of you who are ready to explore tarot relying fully on your own creative authority. It helps to have a standing knowledge of the cards, but that isn't a necessity; there are rituals designed specifically with the brand new reader in mind. My greatest wish is that this becomes an effective resource for folks willing to teach and lead others. May it serve you as the esoteric sandbox it did for myself and my students and clients.

The first few chapters have a singular focus on your relationship with tarot and ritual. Chapter one introduces the magical compatibility of tarot and ritual. Chapter two establishes foundational ideas and practices. Chapter three is an exploration of the cards aimed at developing confidence in your own voice, perceptions, and reality as a reader. Chapter four is a deep dive into tarot's spiritual forces, the major arcana. Chapter five's rituals are deep explorations for the solo diviner. Chapter six focuses on reading rituals for others. Chapters seven through nine explore wider rituals such as annual, group-focused, community building, and formal rituals. Chapter ten helps you create your own rituals. Chapter Eleven is a summary and blessing for your continued growth.

My intention is to combine the wisdom of the high priestess with the rituals of the hierophant. May this union be a catalyst in your own search of tarot's essence for and in your life.

Most important of all, the major premise of these teachings is that all love is a form of magic. Not all magic, however, is a form of love. I caution you to know the difference.

INTRODUCTION

While leading workshops, I often ask students to think of how they would describe their essence by a title and geography. My own response would be, "I am a white horse from the Appalachians." (This exercise will be described fully later for your own use.)

This core identity came from a memory that was formed when I realized there was more to me than being a Catholic girl in central Pennsylvania. While playing with friends during recess on a cold day, I suggested we play make-believe as horses to stay warm. I led them galloping as the white horse leader. They followed behind me as we weaved back and forth. I started to feel sensations like a heavy tail and mane. The more I pretended, the more I believed that I was a white horse. I could feel the thick, warm steam leave my nostrils. The bell signaling the end of recess took me out of this reverie, but I have never forgotten that experience. I knew then that I could be "other" if I moved fully in my heart, body, and imagination. Those childhood days were soon filled with the prescribed rituals of the church.

Church was a constant ritual. These mysteries and structures fueled my curiosity. I took "confessions" in the church when no one else was present except a willing neighborhood kid as my "sinner." Being a tarot reader isn't too far from those earlier confessional rehearsals, where I embodied a role that extended beyond my sense of self. These rituals of my childhood religion had a deep impact on my need to explore divinity through tarot.

There were other mysteries besides those of the Roman Catholic Church. My mom and I were drawn to mystical topics such as phrenology and astrology. She gave me my first tarot deck when I was ten.

At my parochial grade school's show-and-tell, I brought my cards as the object I would share. The lay teacher, who was pregnant at the time, asked for a reading. I suspect now that she did so out of pity for me. I laid down five cards and did my best to tell her what each card said through the picture. I told her that her new baby would only have one small thing wrong with it. She seemed pleased. The reading was almost forgotten until she gave birth to a child with one malformed ear.

While earlier experiences and training by the church provided a sacred environment, dance became my greatest religious form as I grew older. Pretending was not only encouraged in dance, it was accompanied by costumes, music, and lights. I could lose myself in music. Being a fairy, a teapot, or a reindeer was serious business, and these rituals took me beyond the strictures of the church.

I devoted my young adult life to dance. Waitressing tips supported my small wages as a company dancer and teacher. At the restaurant I befriended Jeff, a fellow waiter who was in as bad a shape as me. One night he suggested reading tarot. He laid out his cards dutifully before looking through his book to read the definition for each chosen card. His voice became a soft soundtrack. I locked eyes with a major arcana card, the Magician. Something in me woke up in that moment and never went back to sleep. At a point in my life when I wondered at times if I was going mad, the Magician assured me that I wasn't. The Magician tarot card shows a striking figure in a pose seemingly connecting the sky to earth. Standing behind an altar (warming any Catholic girl's heart) and surrounded in beautiful colors, the Magician suggested a message of comradery, confidence, and support in a vital and creative life.

Jeff gave me my second tarot deck, the Morgan-Greer. It didn't come with a little white book (the "definition cookbook" that usually comes with every deck). I didn't realize there should even be a booklet of definitions. In the early days of tarot's popularity and well before the internet, there were surprisingly few books on tarot. Instead, I studied one card every night by meditating on the image. I began to receive volumes of energy and information from some cards while very little from others. I loved exploring the inner landscapes these cards triggered. My soul was discovering a language, a mirror, a teacher. This was a labyrinth, and I wanted to find its center. I craved more.

I had read in the cards that my true tarot teacher would be in Minneapolis. My brother had moved to the Twin Cities years before so I decided to join him. After I settled in with my brother, I explored the tarot territory. I was disappointed with the traditional methods of teaching that were offered. As I learned the hard way with racquetball, it was a lot less interesting with rules. I started teaching myself using an intuitive approach. Along the way, I became a good tour guide for others who wanted to play and not strictly adhere to the traditional studies of tarot. Both my students and I came to new ways of seeing the cards from our own creative authority. Exercises such as seeing each card as if it were a little movie or theater served as playful and profound explorations. Within a few years, I became the teacher that my tarot reading outlined years beforehand.

Tarot was more than talk though. It felt like a veritable theater with endless plots and characters; verbal explorations could not contain its three-dimensional magic. My good fortune was meeting a powerful web of tarot colleagues, artists, and scholars at tarot conferences. We supported each other in creating theater and dance pieces for the attendees' entertainment and our experimentation. It was incredibly satisfying to go beyond the verbal dimension of tarot. However, there was an essence that remained beyond my reach. Each card speaks to the whole of a world. I wanted to know more about that other world.

Craving that primal experience of being a white horse, I wanted to explore the mysteries through my body. The dance studio has become a laboratory to explore tarot nonverbally. I don't want to imitate tarot, I want to be it. I want to find a way to fully embody this language of images.

This book is a map of sorts of my own journey with tarot. I believe that tarot is a valuable tool in surfacing new worlds. During the writing of this book, our world changed drastically. If you are on the brink of tarot bringing you to a bigger you, may this book serve you well.

Chapter One

THE ALCHEMY OF RITUAL AND TAROT

Historical rituals have great power but are not necessarily superior to those of our own heart's creations. Our own rituals have the power to connect us to something larger than ourselves. Whether you consider this larger dimension to be source, spirit, higher consciousness, or simply our better nature, we can experience this largeness creatively. We are pure energy having a human experience, which is an odd hybrid: temporal yet eternal. The human self craves safety and contentment as its bottom line. The spirit *is* love and *of* love. A life that is spirit-led exists on a whole other scale of satisfaction. What are ways to listen to spirit? How can we be more in tune with this creative facet to consciously shape our lives?

We tend to limit ourselves by the things we can see, smell, hear, taste, and touch. Finding our passion and purpose depends heavily on bringing these senses to new levels of perception. Imagination and creativity are key ingredients in sensing the unseen, hearing the small voice, and acting from one's gut. We can transform our senses using symbols, music, art, movement, and storytelling. These creative forms help us build a greater connection to ourselves, our purpose, to each other, and hopefully something much bigger.

Tarot and ritual are forms that hold the best of symbols, art, and storytelling. Each has their own strengths in terms of surfacing messages and mystery. Together, however, these two forms can produce an undeniable alchemy, a transformational process of turning the ordinary into the extraordinary. Traditionally speaking, alchemy was a process to convert base metals into gold or silver. Tarot and ritual together do much the same. Their coupling can transform ideas, feelings, and understanding to create new realities.

Ritual is intention and action. It can be as small as a handshake when greeting someone. This gesture's intention is to welcome the other. The action is touching their hand in a prescribed manner. On a larger scale, such as a funeral ceremony, the intention is to honor a loved one's life and call on the ancestors for their swift return home. The action is the text, song, and stories of their community and culture.

Rituals tend to grow in strength through repetition. Consider for instance that habits can be rituals. They are repetitive actions but often without intention. The simple addition of intent can transform these repetitive acts to spirit-led action:

- Brushing your teeth—letting go of harsh words
- Sweeping/shoveling—asking for the protection of your space
- Making your bed—gratefulness for another day
- Mailing bills—blessing the Creative Unknown for your prosperity

Rituals are conscious invitations for mystery and synchronicity. They are hearty road posts for life's significant events: graduations, weddings, or an initiation. Transitions are often powerful times of vulnerability and change.

Rituals can hold the power of transformation to release destructive beliefs, open perceptions to new ways of being, or enable finding one's way through a tumultuous time. They are containers for the fragility inherent in the beginning and end of a relationship and other crossroads of life. Ritual can bond people through creating a sense of belonging and connection.

Tarot is a strong, visual language that speaks to the imagination through a specific structure of symbols, titles, and numbers. As a graphic storyteller, tarot acts as a reflection for the individual as well as the culture. While the stories of tarot originated in the Italian Renaissance, they continue to gather power for our hearts and minds even today. Tarot is a blueprint for being fully human.

Whether one believes the deck to be an effective synchronistic tool without a supernatural edge, a powerful way to predict patterns, or a mirror into one's unconscious, tarot has held its ground in terms of shifting perceptions and practice through the centuries. Not bad for a set of picture cards, eh?

Ritual's symbolic action and tarot's symbolic language form a unique kind of theater. The stage audience member suspends disbelief as the initial curtain rises. The ritual participant does much the same by declaring sacred space. A ritual is often enhanced much like any stage show with lighting, music, text, and people taking on certain roles. The script is the ritual's outline of a sequence of actions and/or tarot's narrative. Costumes enhance the players' significance. There may be choreography or stylized movement in both forms such as the lighting of candles, the trancelike sound of shuffling cards, or the placing of cards in formation. The goal is to fully engage in the process of this pretend time and place. If done well, the perceptions that result from experiencing a created reality whether onstage or in ceremony can produce magical results. The ability to allow new perceptions is the height of magic.

Tarot can act in a number of ways in combination with ritual. It helps one focus on the true intention for the ritual, as well as designing the structure. It can capture the mystery during the ritual by delivering the message or action needed. It can clarify the messages received during the process.

Tarot ritual practices provide tangible benefits, allowing one to:

- Become a better neutral observer in one's life and the lives of others
- Honor passages of time for needed integration of known and unknown changes
- Receive essential information
- Use imagery and art to cut through the mental chatter/restrictions
- Activate synchronicity

Within this book, tarot combined with ritual will cover a huge spectrum of ideas and structures. Tarot rituals can range from the simplicity of a basic spread to the elaborateness of using the cards ritualistically in a wedding ceremony. Exercises and rituals are provided for the solitary practitioner, groups of four or more, those conducting readings for others, as well as for seasonal transitions and special events.

Whether magic is perceived as real or imagined, it is a potent change agent. Exploring and creating new realities through tarot rituals is the goal of this book. In Jungian psychology, this magic is called the active imagination—a meditative technique to surface the ideas of the unconscious. The tai chi master T. T. Liang refers to this essence in his book of the same title as *Imagination Becomes Reality*. A familiar phrase in describing a way to practice confidence in oneself until it is a trusted skill is "fake it 'till you make it."

My term is the "Power of Pretend." Pretending doesn't preclude the desired result. Pretending gives one freedom from rational limitations. It has the effect of dismantling the need to censor. It is a holy act. It is the first door to an entire corridor leading to endless creative potential. It is often the very permission to not be real that allows one to become more real.

Trust your curiosity as you explore these rituals and suggestions. Your first suggested ritual: always tap this book three times before opening it. I'll tell you about this later although you may figure it out before then ... or simply pretend.

Summary

The characteristics and functions of both tarot and ritual are explored. The benefits of practicing either are plentiful. Together, however, they create a form that can transcend time and space. As a vehicle for magic, the tarot ritual surfaces hidden realities through new perceptions. The Power of Pretend is introduced as an effective technique to use throughout the book. It is a shortcut to imagination and possibilities.

Chapter Two

HELPFUL FUNDAMENTALS

If everything is energy, how do you define who we are as energetic beings? Do you believe we are spirits having a human experience? If not, what is your understanding? How do you define that larger sense of all of us? Is it love, spirit, source, creativity, a collective wisdom? These questions cannot be brushed over if you plan to work with tarot and ritual. You need to know the ground you stand on before you fly and land with effectiveness. Your own creative authority is needed to enter mystery effectively. This is your unique connection and understanding of spirit, source, or other. We "practice" being spirit. It is a practice because it is challenging to consider our "self" in a dimension beyond our bodies. Releasing into our own creative authority is an act of love. A spiritual practice can further support one's creativity, compassion, and cultivation of resiliency. Going within oneself and bringing those inner landscapes into the world is a rich dance of loving life. A practice makes all the difference between aimlessly reacting to the road before us and walking on a road to a desired destination. Following your own creative authority means taking the ultimate responsibility for your spiritual well-being beyond templates of right and wrong.

Becoming a full co-creator of reality is contingent on taking responsibility for your own life. Your state of well-being is a primary task. This requires continuous development of resilience, self-awareness, and compassion while nurturing a curious outlook. Maintaining a regular ritual of spiritual hygiene for yourself and your living space creates a balancing neutrality that contributes greatly to a sense of well-being. One travels through the spheres of mystery if connected to oneself with love and support. From this point onward, this source will be referred to as the "Creative Unknown," but you are encouraged to name and claim it for yourself.

As spirit and human, we are of two worlds. This intersection is an entire realm of possibility—a world existing between the worlds. Before one begins a casual exploration of ritual and divination, be advised to enter this liminal space mindfully and with intention. Boundaries are needed in all worlds.

The practice called "grounding" describes a large spectrum of techniques that allow you to fully enter a liminal space mentally, emotionally, and physically. A few basic suggestions are given in this book, and there are numerous outside resources available regarding breath work, movement, and release of linear time to aid in this pivotal transition. Divination work that causes overthinking and depletion can be the result of a faulty or non-existent grounding ritual.

This simple ritual is helpful before doing any other rituals or exercises in this book.

Grounding Ritual

Close your eyes and slowly scan your body. Is there anything that needs attention? For example, if there is a tight spot in your neck or shoulders, some stretching is in order. Listen to your body in any desired adjustments of posture or breath.

Find a comfortable sitting position with your feet on the ground. Breathe slowly, silently, and softly. Envision each inhale as a rich color. For example, use the Power of Pretend to imagine that you are breathing in the color blue. The blue represents the form of your spirit. Each breath of color fills your body. Each exhale is the release of all that you do not need, such as worries or concerns. Imagine the exhales as gray or black smoke.

Envision the rich color of your inhales expanding through and beyond your body, surrounding it in all directions by about a foot. As it expands beyond the outline of your body it is as if your body is now within a huge egg of sorts. Open to the Creative Unknown as you open your eyes. You are refreshed and awake.

Now, let us enter the mysteries of tarot. If you are brand new to tarot, I encourage you to consider working through my first book, *Psychic Tarot: Using Your Natural Abilities to Read the Cards*. It describes basic intuitive principles for the solo reader. I have also included other tarot resources in the suggested reading list found at the back of this book. We won't be going into detail for the beginner reader, but do not be discouraged because basic concepts will be provided. There is much to gain for any curious reader, new or seasoned.

Tarot is a language of images. It holds the possibilities of countless narratives within and between the seventy-eight cards. Tarot has three families: the greater forces of life in the twenty-two major arcana, the everyday magic of life in the forty minor arcana, and the human portrayals represented by the sixteen court cards of the minor arcana. From its Latin root *arcanum*, "arcana" means "secrets." As the "greater secrets," the major arcana represent the mystery and changing forces of our greater nature. These can be viewed as guiding forces, different aspects of the Creative Unknown, teachers, or crossroads. The Fool begins everything as number zero. The journey continues all the way through to the last major arcana—the World. Each of these cards has a descriptive title such as "the Empress" or "Judgement." They are most likely denoted by roman numerals as well, depending on the deck.

The minor arcana reflect the mysteries of everyday living. The minor arcana suits, commonly separated into suits of swords, wands, cups, and pentacles (but sometimes described differently) are much like playing cards numbered ace through 10. Each suit symbolizes an element that makes up life itself—air, fire, water, and earth. As we are spirits having a human experience, these four elements are the gifts of life, its very substance and magic. They are therefore tarot's foundational backbone.

The "royalty" of the four suits are the sixteen court cards. These are most often labeled page, knight, queen, and king within the Rider-Waite-Smith system. The court cards represent the various roles each of us play, in addition to the people in our lives. Another way to read the court cards is as their pure elemental energy or traditional position: the page is the risk and inexperience of managing their element, the knight is the focus and action of the warrior, the queen is the visionary and overseer of the people, and the king is the commitment and responsibility of a leader. Many consider the court cards to be the most challenging to read. We are comfortable with seeing larger archetypes such as the major arcana and the scenes of everyday life as in the minor arcana. The court cards reflect the human mirrors, which may cause projection and judgment. With time and experience, however, the court cards can actually expand our view of how we see ourselves and others.

The elemental world has been observed in rituals for centuries. It is an integral part of many religions and spiritual beliefs. The annual cycle of the seasons, otherwise known as the Wheel of the Year, is a metaphorical platform of life that observes all the elements. A common template of the directions within the medicine wheels of earth-based religions is as follows:

- East as air
- South as fire
- West as water
- North as earth

This organic structure reflects a number of core rhythms: the seasons, the ages of a person, and the transformation of day into night. It is a sacred clock of sorts.

All beginnings start in the east. The swords represent this element of air. The swords suit denotes power, thought, and communication. Everything starts with thought. The potential of the mind is as open and spacious as the sky. It is the power of perception, consciousness, and awareness.

The south direction brings the heat. The wood of the wands (or rods) builds all fires—including those of imagination, sensuality, and expression in the world. Just as in any fulfilling creative process, one can be totally consumed as when watching a fire burn. It is a dance of movement beyond time.

Water is to the west. This is the home of the cups (also known as chalices). The cup symbolizes our heart. It can process an ocean of feelings and vision. Emotions are represented by all forms of water—solid, fluid, and vapor. It can symbolize ice for when we are wounded, steam as anger, or a river of flowing emotions. Without this connection to ourselves and others, life can easily become rote or mechanical.

The north direction is the home of the pentacles (or disks or coins). The pentacles correspond to form and the substance of matter—of earth itself. Matter matters! The pentacles symbolize natural resources and forms of time, money, focus, energy, and health.

Tarot's strong symbolic nature expressed through the elements and the Creative Unknown, along with the sacred theater of ritual, provide the platform for a great catalyst for change.

Let us now focus on ritual, a term used throughout this book. Ritual can be as simple as doing a tarot spread, or as complex as performing introspective work such as meditation for one person. Formal structures and observances for a number of people are also explored. This entire book leads to the rituals you create to generate the necessary, dynamic shifts you want in your life.

Unlike an exercise or study, a ritual requires careful attention to:

1. *Intention:* What is wanted? What is the request, desired outcome, or needed clarification?
2. *Form:* How will you receive information? Will it be through a tarot reading, meditation, planned exercise, channeled reading, or other method?
3. *Download:* This is the response from the Creative Unknown, the answer through which messages, insights, and patterns are revealed.
4. *Integration:* How will you integrate the received insight into your everyday life?

Ritual is a creative act to "play out" a specific intent and all great magic starts with a solid intention. It is important to fully sense and clarify your intentions. Why are you doing this? What do you hope will happen? What do you think you need from the Creative Unknown? For example, say you want to find a new job. Your intention could be, "I work in a job where I enjoy the people I work with and for, earning a life-sustaining income." You want to stay inspired and hopeful during this search.

After clarifying the intention, take some time to let it cook. Stay open for additional patterns, images, or insights. Stay true to the process as you remain unattached to the outcome. Make room for the Creative Unknown to "play out" with you. Using the Power of Pretend, imagine that you are a sacred, trained magician who easily channels the beauty and power of love. Write, meditate, dream, divine; and work with an open, receptive mind, heart, and body. Allow imagination and trust to take over. Say yes to all ideas initially. Only when you have gathered all that you wish, begin the process of paring down to the best ideas for the ritual. Trust that what needs to surface will. Mystery isn't directed, it is invited.

Keep in mind that time is fluid between the worlds. This shift from linear time into a sense of circular or endless time is itself a sacred act. We all have experienced this sense when lost in conversation with a good friend, doing something we love, or on vacation. This sense of "all time" is sacred time. Opening to one's Creative Unknown allows linear time to disappear into a web where past, present, and future are imagined. Act as if this is possible; it will greatly aid in allowing time to open.

Ritual is ultimately a structure for the Creative Unknown to be sensed or heard. The heartbeat of the ritual, the desired intention, needs a structure or form. Form follows function. The following functions will help create a significant ritual.

What: The intention is most likely a request, a prayer of sorts, or an honoring. Find the text, tools, and props needed to express it fully. There is no right or wrong choice in the selection. What makes the intention real for you?

How: Set a block of time for silence to receive responses and insights. The time set aside for listening is often the transformative point of the ritual. After the insight has been requested, wait for a message or download. This could be information that you sense or a shift in perspective. Choosing tarot cards is a viable way to receive messages. Afterward, imagine leaving sacred time by closing doors to re-enter linear time.

When: Whether you follow lunar cycles or a specific anniversary, it helps to set a specific time and date for your ritual. Creating a specific date and duration contributes to a ritual's potency. Dedicating a specific time minimizes the mental chatter that remains in linear time.

Where: The space to be considered is both literal and energetic. There may be a specific geographical area suited for the ritual. The chosen space needs to offer safety and privacy. Beauty and room to move about are helpful enhancements, though rituals can be created any-where—even in your car.

Who: Ritual is an intimate act. Invite human and divine participants who are supportive of you and your intent, e.g., a beloved family member who has passed or a Divine Ally who brings a sense of clarity and peace. Relationships with these two groups creates a sense of connec-tion to that larger sense of self. None of us are truly alone. Trusting the Creative Unknown in your understanding of it brings all that is yours to you.

Other: Consider all aspects of any good theater—lighting, costume, staging, directions, a script, and sound. Bigger is not always better—a simple bell or vase of flowers can do wonders.

Calling the Circle Ritual

A strong foundation using tarot in ritual is grounding oneself, opening the four directions or quarters to create sacred space, listening for messages from the Creative Unknown, and closing the quarters. This structure is in the fol-lowing basic ritual and is the basic template used throughout the rest of this book.

The Setup

Carefully choose your ceremonial space, and then signify the four quarters by marking the true directions of the space in some manner. This can be as simple as lighting one candle each for east, south, west, and north. Altars for each quarter with symbols or objects corresponding to that specific direction—e.g., a beautiful bowl of water placed in the west, or feathers placed in the east—are visually effective.

Designate the center of the circle—an area to meditate, sit, listen, and receive information from the Creative Unknown. The lion's share of the ritual will be activated in this center area. Since you might be sitting for fifteen minutes or more, a meditation mat or chair could be helpful for comfort. Your deck of cards could be placed in the center for easy access. A soundtrack of soothing music or other sounds deepens the suspension of reality. You might prefer a timer to relax and surrender to receiving the messages of the ritual. Include any visual mementos, written intentions that you may read aloud, or poetry for a verbal expression to the Creative Unknown.

The Ritual

First and foremost, it is essential to enter any sacred space feeling connected to your body, mind, and spirit. The Grounding ritual (page 12) is an example. You could also envision beams of colored light traveling down the crown of your head and coming up from the earth through your feet. It is necessary to shift your energy from day-to-day responsibilities and demands in order to prepare to enter a different sense of time and space.

Move clockwise to each direction starting with the east, then moving to the south, west, and north. Invite the loving guardians—your Creative Unknown in the form of Divine Allies and Beloved Ancestors—of each quarter. If you wish, light a candle in each quarter. Invite, call, and/or welcome any loving presence needed for this ritual. Imagine the element itself such as a strong wind in the east, the heat of a fire in the south, the hypnotic rhythm of an ocean in the west, or the scent of moss in the north. Use the Power of Pretend to open portals where all love exists in all states of being and possibilities.

After the quarters have been acknowledged and invited, take your seat in the center of the ritual circle with your request or intention. The highlight of the ritual is sitting quietly in the center for a certain amount of time to receive any image, message, or knowledge from the Creative Unknown. Pull tarot cards during or after the meditation for future insights. For example, you could pull three cards corresponding to the past, present, and future. You could interpret the cards within the ritual or gather them to interpret within a few days.

When there is a sense of completeness or a designated time has passed, move counterclockwise starting with north to thank the presence of that direction. Blowing out the candles of the quarters or ringing a bell is a satisfying release. Let the ritual settle in your heart. Reflect and record the messages received through the chosen cards or energetic downloads.

Summary

Concepts such as being spirit-led, one's creative authority, and the Creative Unknown all blend beautifully with the action of being a co-creator of your life. The Power of Pretend allows us to dive into mystery and potential. Separately, tarot and ritual are potent symbolic storytelling devices. Together, they form an alchemy that has the potential to enter the veils of mystery for change and transformation. Both forms brilliantly use the four elements as life's foundation.

Chapter Three

FOR THE
SOLO READER

This chapter's focus is using tarot as a primary tool for ritual, whether for divination, personal exploration, celebration, or honoring an event. The various suggestions will help develop your unique voice. Ideas are given for choosing a primary deck and additional decks to be used in rituals. After blessing your primary deck, the One Card ritual is a method that can be used to discover the essence of each card. A deeper exploration of the aspects of tarot families may be achieved through the use of the Essence spread. The One Aspect ritual and the popular Card of the Day ritual can both create structures of deep spiritual practices. These easy-to-use spreads and techniques are offered for the beginning reader as well as the seasoned ones. Feel free to edit and add to these rituals to your heart's desire. Keep in mind that you need to discover what is real for you. Leave the paradigm of right-wrong behind and remember that the process of divination starts from within.

Energy is the basic material of all of life and is the language of spirit as well. We read energy through patterns and pattern recognition is key in this endeavor. Perceiving patterns through tarot's imagery and art is a lifetime discovery. Even though there are centuries-old definitions for each card, deeper patterns of meaning will surface with or without that knowledge.

Tarot is a living art form. Start the relationship with this collection of images by trusting what you see *and* sense. You want to develop the ability to speak fluently of image. Images can literally open portals of energy and time. The more you "listen" to images, the more adept you will be at "speaking" images.

There are ways to strengthen your imagery language:

- Start linking random images together to create a story. Three is plenty for a plot. For example, using one image from Instagram, a billboard, and a magazine in a classical story structure: "Once upon a time (first image), this happened (second image), and in the end (third image)."
- Turn off the audio of any show or program to decipher the messages by observing body language, colors, symbols, etc. Better yet, change the program's settings to a language you don't know.
- Create a paragraph of social media "language" using only images and GIFs.
- Play and work with coloring books.

To look, listen, and sense an image's energy is a primary step in seeing a bigger pattern.

Let's focus on becoming the seer. Through the Power of Pretend, imagine that you have had previous training in the intuitive arts. You have learned from those much wiser than yourself. Through their teachings, you have become adept in trusting your sixth sense to serve yourself and many others. You have great skill in witnessing others while staying open to the possibilities from between the worlds. The insights you receive enhance their lives. As you explore tarot, know that you are remembering glorious training and support from another incarnation. If you don't sense other lifetimes as a seer, pretend that you, the cards, and all else are energy. For example, imagine light or color coming from your hands or from the cards.

In time, a number of tarot decks may serve various needs for certain states of being or special occasions. One may use specific decks while reading for others. Other decks may be for the reader's private use only. There are decks that work well in both settings. You will know what is a good fit by instant preference or trial and error. For now, however, commit to one deck while learning tarot. This deck will become your primary instrument, much like someone might start their music education using the piano. Once the basics of music are learned, such as reading music and practicing scales, those skills can be transferable to other instruments. Likewise, with tarot, learning with a primary deck sets a foundational understanding. All additional decks you might use afterward will be variations of this primary language, much like a musician playing other instruments after starting with the piano.

When choosing a deck, look for one whose art and philosophy resonate strongly with your own tastes and beliefs. Tarot cards come in nearly every sense of artistic style and cosmology one can imagine. Enjoy the process of choosing a deck that appeals to both your sense of art and spirituality. Illustrated pictorial scenes for each of the minor arcana cards are highly recommended for tarot beginners. The imagery needs to portray a scene, such as the Four of Pentacles showing a person holding onto four pentacles tightly, which will convey a different message than just four pentacles. It can be confusing working with a deck that only shows multiple objects instead of a scene.

Tarot Rituals uses the Rider-Waite-Smith system as its base. Some adaptations will be needed if you choose the Thoth, Marseilles, or independent decks that have alternative structures and images.

Got your primary deck? It is time to claim your deck as your tool. Keep in mind that doing the Grounding ritual (pg 12) will be beneficial before any other suggested ritual or casual exploration.

Anointing the Deck Ritual

As you remove the plastic wrap or covering of the deck, thank all those who labored to bring this deck to your hands. Remove the deck from its box. Find a suitable bag, pouch, or wooden box to keep it in unless you love its original container. Close your eyes as you hold the deck. Welcome the spirit of this deck.

After any feelings have settled, look at each card as though you are meeting a good friend for the first time. When finished, shuffle or mix the entire deck. Randomly choose one card facedown after asking, "How do you and I best serve the Creative Unknown?" Look at the card and give permission for your initial judgments ("this card is good/bad/not what I wanted," "yikes what does this mean?," etc.). After this initial response, go deeper. Take note of the initial action words that come to mind. Perhaps you sense a great sense of peace in the card, so the action word might be "flow" or "relax." These verbs are clues into the essence of this deck. Gather the cards together. Bless them before putting them into their home.

With used decks, you may want to add an additional charge such as placing them on a table that catches moonlight or sunlight, run the cards through the smoke of your favorite herbs, or sprinkle them with Florida Water (a light cologne used for spiritual cleansings).

Your first deck may have its own special magic. I use my original deck for ritual purposes only. For instance, I buried Kiki, my Siamese familiar, with the Queen of Wands card. I also used certain cards for an image board created to become pregnant. It worked.

For the purpose of this book, it would help to have a deck based on the Rider-Waite-Smith system. It is also recommended to have a couple of decks that you can use primarily in ritual settings. Have at least one that can be put on the floor or on an outside surface if you don't want your principal deck to go through wear and tear. It also helps to have a deck that can be physically altered, such as using parts of cards in a collage, burning or burying them, or giving a card to another as a blessing.

With the primary deck chosen and blessed, it is time to meet the seventy-eight storyboards. The following structure is a method to approach each card mentally, emotionally, physically, and spiritually.

You initially see your tarot cards for the first time only once. Explorations such as the following ritual deserve to be recorded to remember your first impression. Dedicate one large journal for these tarot insights. Consider a journal that has the capacity to grow with additional pages, such as a three-ring binder. Each card could have its own section. In addition, tracking significant events, signposts, and the date within your deck's own book of definitions can offer invaluable insights and reveal a larger pattern over time.

Entering the Card Ritual

Devote time for observation, research, embodiment, writing, and meditation for each card. Record all significant findings and the date. Start with the Ace of Swords through the King of Swords. Repeat with the wands, cups, and pentacles. Save the major arcana for a great finale.

Observation

What is your immediate judgment? Is this card good, negative, scary, confusing, beautiful, or powerful? Now breathe to go beyond your first impression. Where is the main charge or energy of the picture depicted? What thought, memory, message, or idea is being activated within?

Research

Without going too far down the rabbit hole for this first round, find traditional meanings within a few key words. I highly recommend world-renowned tarot master Rachel Pollack's *Seventy-Eight Degrees of Tarot Wisdom*, which includes a thorough list of historical meanings for each card. Pick meanings that resonate strongly for you.

Embodiment

Your body has an animal wisdom that will greatly enhance the way you perceive a card. Select one aspect or gesture of the card. For example, focus on the stationary pose of the Knight of Pentacles. Imitate the pose and expression. Look in the same direction. Start with this gesture or feeling of the card. Close your eyes. Find it in your body. Do you feel it in your chest, throat, or somewhere else? Invite the energy of the card within. Say a key word of this card out loud three times. For example, for this particular knight, you may feel "waiting, waiting, waiting." Move in slow, steady increments. Go beyond your mind. Listen to what your body will do with this movement and key word. Become an internal observer to the mover within. This nonverbal exploration may uncover surprising insights.

Writing

This is my variation of an incredibly profound exercise designed by Rachel Pollack:

1. List everything you literally see, including the environment, the type of people, animals, etc.
2. List everything you sense, such as the figure's state of being, what may have happened right before this moment, or the general mood.
3. Write about the emerging story seen and sensed in the card as a fairy tale starting with, "Once upon a time …" Keep it simple and fantastic.
4. How is this story currently applicable in your life?

Meditation

Set a timer for fifteen minutes. Sit with the card's image in your mind. See the two-dimensional scene of the card expanding slowly in all directions to encompass a larger world. Stay unattached to any outcome. Allow your curiosity to follow anything that surfaces. How does this card become a part of a bigger world? How does it describe or frame some part of your life? How do you relate to this scene?

After viewing this card from these different perspectives, make sure to include what surprised you the most. These moments have a lasting impact on your understanding.

A helpful idea as you discover your own tarot voice is keeping in mind that the very bones of tarot are elemental in nature. This language of images is expressed through the elements: earth, air, water, and fire. Think of yourself as being comprised of all four elements. The elements naturally interact with each other and are the foundation of greater forces of love—the major arcana.

The Tarot Families

Swords: *Ace through King*—Air—East

Wands: *Ace through King*—Fire—South

Cups: *Ace through King*—Water—West

Pentacles: *Ace through King*—Earth—North

Court cards: *Page, Knight, Queen, King*—Humanity

Major Arcana: *0 through 21*—Forces of the Creative Unknown

The following are rituals designed for each of these families. These rituals will provide your own experience as the Magician. As the Magician, you stand at an altar with all four elements to channel the energy between earth and sky.

You can do each ritual for its own sake or do them all to culminate in the Essence spread, which is explained later in this chapter. Record which card is chosen during the meditation(s). The Essence spread is particularly effective during seasonal turning points, birthdays, and New Year's.

Recommendations of physical settings are provided to give you a sense of space, using either actual or metaphorical locations. Facing the direction of the element itself helps with the flow of energy. Dedicate a space for an altar for this series of rituals. This could simply be a table or a place that is defined by candles for each direction.

Remember, the Grounding ritual (on page 12) is a necessary step into sacred time.

Swords—Ritual of the Mind

Separate all the swords from the deck. Shuffle only this suit. Lay them face-down in a circle either around you or on a surface within reach.

SETTING

Imagine being on top of a hill facing east, looking into a huge sky. Sit quietly and close your eyes. Envision a large stone. Within this stone is your buried sword. This is the sword that incarnated with you from the very beginning. You might only see its hilt showing. When ready to hold your power, responsibility, and full ability to communicate authentically, pull the sword from the rock. The sword may not leave the stone easily, especially if you have any doubt or expectations. When the stone does release it, however, you feel a surge of energy run through your arm and into your whole body. Lay this sword onto the eastern part of the altar.

Open your eyes. Randomly choose a card from the circle by sensing which energy most matches the energy of the sword. Look at the card. This card reflects an important message about your current power and ability to communicate effectively. What is this message? Write it down. If this message is not readily understood, take notes of your initial impressions.

Wands—Ritual of Expression

Separate all the wands from the deck. Shuffle only this suit. Lay them facedown in a circle either around you or on a surface within reach.

SETTING

Imagine you are facing south, sitting by a fire or a burning candle. Creating and maintaining a real fire during the entire ritual is wildly helpful. A candle or a small cauldron will work.

Sit quietly and close your eyes. If not by a real fire, envision one. Watch the flames burn away linear time and concerns. Within the flames, visualize your wand—the wand that incarnated with you from the beginning. This wand is the power of the Tree of Life which is never destroyed. It is your life force. When ready to experience full sensuality, creativity, and true identity, call to the wand to come to you. The fire feels oddly fluid, and the wand fits your hand perfectly. You feel a vitality and connection to earth emanating through your whole body. Lay this wand on the southern part of the altar.

Open your eyes and find the wand's energetic equal from the wands cards laying facedown in front of you. This card speaks to the current way you express your magic and your unique essence in the world. What insight surfaced?

Cups—Ritual of the Heart of Vision

Once you separate all the cups from the deck, shuffle only this suit. Place them facedown in a circle either around you or on a surface within reach.

SETTING

Imagine you are facing west, near a river or a fountain. Soaking in a hot bath or swimming beforehand would be helpful.

Sit quietly and close your eyes. Envision sitting near a body of water. The cup brings with it the depth and expansion of deep waters. Imagine hearing the water and let it lull you into a calm state. When ready to accept a full vision without censoring, call for the cup that incarnated with you. After you call, reach out your arm to receive the cup from this body of water. As you hold this cup, feel your heart and intuition expand with ease. Place this cup onto the western part of the altar.

Open your eyes and select one card that matches the vibration of the cup you held. This card reflects the way you currently love and teach others how to love you.

Pentacles—Ritual of Form

Once you have separated all the pentacles from the deck, shuffle only this suit. Lay them facedown in a circle either around you or on a surface within reach.

SETTING

Imagine facing north, lightly holding a crystal of your choice, or sitting amid a grove of trees.

Sit quietly and close your eyes. Envision being on a mound of earth. Let the earth completely support you. Release all stress about money, work, health, and time. As you lie there, slowly become aware of healing energy coming to you from above and below.

Your body absorbs it readily. Stress dissipates and falls away. When ready, call the pentacle that arrived during your incarnation. This five-pointed crystal will bring a sense of wholeness and vitality. The crystal is the abundance of this planet. Place the crystal on the northern point of the altar.

Open your eyes to randomly select the pentacle card most fitting the crystal. It brings a message from your body that is purposeful and sustaining for you. Record your insights.

Court Cards—Ritual of Persona

Select all the court cards (the pages, knights, queens, and kings) from the deck, regardless of suit. Shuffle them together. Lay them facedown in a circle either around you or on a surface within reach. You will choose one of these cards after the visualization of different groups of visitors.

SETTING

Imagine you are in an empty amphitheater or park.

Sit quietly and close your eyes. The first group of folks to envision are those who have strongly influenced you, whether alive or passed. Recalling a memory of yours, these individuals start to arrive in a circle around you. Allow all who come to mind. Does anyone have a message for you? Listen carefully for the messages you most need to hear right now. When finished, thank them before they depart.

Gently shift your perceptions to those people whom you have influenced. Envision your life by chapters. Who stands out in those specific times? Don't be surprised if there are people whom you don't recognize. Receive their blessings. Thank them as they depart.

Next, invite all of the aspects that represent the various roles you play in your life. These include selves such as daughter/son, parent, sibling, worker, citizen, lover, seeker, etc. Be unattached in how they may present themselves. Envision the aspects of your former selves as well. Is there a role or aspect that stands out among the rest? If so, take in their message carefully. Thank these parts of you as they depart.

The last group to envision are the sixteen court figures. They enter your vision according to their position in the hierarchy. The pages enter first as young apprentices. The knights make their way to stand guard. The queens enter with presence and power. The kings are last to enter the circle to stand near their queens. Do you have any resonance with them? Is there a message to be heard if one stands out? Are you curious about one in particular? Thank them as they depart.

Consider these four groups of personas: those with great influence in your life, those you have influenced, the roles you enact in your life, and the court cards themselves. Using the Power of Pretend, imagine inviting the one persona which represents your current greatest growth. Have no expectations of the one you come face-to-face with. Allow a dialogue to unfold between you.

Open your eyes. Select the card from the court cards that feels like the persona aspect that surfaced. Place it to the right of the center of the altar.

Major Arcana—Ritual of the Creative Unknown

Have a list of the major arcana to read aloud nearby. Separate all the major arcana from the deck and shuffle them. Lay them facedown in a circle either around you or on a surface within reach.

SETTING

Imagine a temple-like structure or labyrinth with an altar nearby. Sit quietly and close your eyes. Envision standing in a large space outdoors that is real or imaginary. Stand, if you are able, and feel the sky with its warm sun or shining moon and stars. A beam of light enters through the crown of your head. The light travels down through your spine to suffuse your entire body. The light overflows from your body to fill the entire space around you. You are immersed in light.

Read the major arcana list slowly out loud. One by one, the major arcana gather in a circle around you. They may appear as their card depictions, as a color, or light, or as a specific animal or symbolic representation. Become aware of how the energy shifts with each arrival. These are all loving aspects of the Creative Unknown.

Open to the current crossroads in your life. How would you characterize your recent themes or state of being? Which major arcana sheds much needed light? What is necessary to learn or assimilate?

As you turn your focus to the questions of necessary guidance, one major arcana will make itself known by stepping forward. The others disappear.

Enjoy this major arcana's presence. Remain open for any message or dialogue. Open your eyes and randomly select the card that feels as if it holds the same essence of this major arcana. Place it left of the center of your altar.

For those new to tarot, congratulations! You have just chosen the cards for your first spread. The Essence spread is a powerful inventory of your current integration of the elements and spirit. This spread is a helpful reset button.

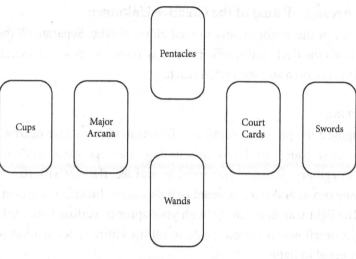

Essence Spread

Essence Spread

The Essence spread is the culmination of the cards placed on your altar during the preceding suit rituals. The chosen cards are facing up. Approach the reading as if you are a high priestess—curious, skilled, and open to messages without judgment. Take your time considering the message of each card and of the whole picture. What are your strengths? What feels off-balance? Date and record your findings and whether or not the divine communication is fully understood or felt at this time. These messages may certainly become crystal clear later.

The elemental rituals and the Essence spread lend themselves to learning the language of tarot in a visceral way that engages all the senses. There are many kinds of knowledge such as logic, wisdom, and physical sensations. All are worth developing to a new level but especially in unison with each other.

One Aspect Ritual

Another ritual culminating in a spread is the One Aspect ritual. It is recommended to set a time limit to prevent overthinking. The first section is about forty minutes. Afterward, the spread will need to be viewed on and off for about two hours.

Take five minutes to list any life aspects that have been taking up considerable focus or energy lately. Narrow the list to one item for additional insight or action.

Give yourself ten minutes to declare a strong intention regarding this particular aspect. Know which insight or responses would move the needle. Examples:

I wish to release any belief that there is not enough time, money, love, etc.
I want to be loved well and in a reciprocal way with a partner.
I ask for insight in stopping self-sabotaging behaviors.

Set a timer for ten minutes. Rather than choosing a card randomly, go through the deck to look at all the cards' images. Choose all cards that provoke a strong reaction or have some sort of effect upon you, including desired responses, thoughts, feelings, and deepest fears regarding the intention. Set aside the pile of cards that have little or no impact at all.

Set the timer for another ten minutes and carefully go through the chosen cards. Select only those cards that you feel are essential to a new understanding. Allow the Creative Unknown to guide this choice. Pretend that a Divine Ally or former teacher literally directs your selection.

Now set the timer for five minutes. Lay out the remaining cards into a pleasing pattern and preferred sequence. This could be a long line or a circle with one card in the center if nothing else comes to mind. These cards combine as the Creative Unknown's response to your intention. Be creative but keep it simple. Now it's time to let it simmer. Don't try to interpret anything at this time or give it any thought at all for the next few hours (or possibly overnight).

When ready, return to the reading. Record all initial impressions and perspectives. Resist looking up others' definitions. Allow the images to speak directly to your heart. Sit quietly and let the information flow. Hold on to nothing. Remain engaged and open. Allow the messages to surface unimpeded from making sense. At times, a reading works very much like a dream: it may not make sense, but there is a strongly felt narrative. What is the Creative Unknown's response to your intention?

Card of the Day (COTD) Ritual

Another ritual you can use is popular among tarot folk. It is the Card of the Day ritual, commonly known as COTD.

Magic is only as good as the intention behind it, so set a general intention to use for this ritual each day. My intention—"How do I serve love today?"—is quite effective. This ritual can easily evolve into a spiritual practice.

Shuffle all the cards in the deck while thinking of your intention and choose a card randomly. Stay aware of this card on and off throughout the day.

Perception is reality. Trusting your own perception is a huge step in finding your tarot language. If you are brand new to tarot, resist reading definitions until the evening. Before going to the "authorities," pay attention to where and how the message of this card surfaced during the day. For example, the Eight of Wands was chosen. It gave you a sense of excitement and rapid movement. You receive an email that your book proposal was accepted. Record all highlights before reading any definitions.

Consider marking your significant events or experiences in the deck's definition book as well as your own journal. Over time, you will see a pattern associated with particular cards. A simple title and date will show layers of certain cards throughout the years. Thinking and perceiving in tarot is the foundation for building an organic language over time.

With daily use, the same card may surface over and over. This is a memo from the Creative Unknown to go deeper. This card would certainly be a good candidate for another round of the Entering the Card ritual (pg 25). The new insights gathered may reveal some secrets, but the following ritual will aid in diving deeper into a card that seems to want your full attention.

Bears Repeating Ritual

When one specific card shows up over and over, the Bears Repeating ritual will help you find the card's specific message for you. Its constant appearance calls for stronger introspection.

For example, say you continue to draw the Five of Wands. Take a closer look at this insistent card. List all the aspects that you see in the image. Where do you sense a lot of charge? It helps to break down the image of the card into smaller units. There is no right or wrong way to do this.

Shuffle and choose a card to represent each of the card's aspects. In the instance of the Five of Wands, you might pull a card to symbolize each of the five wands.

Write the first word or phrase that comes to mind when looking at these cards. From this written list, create a step of action that can be taken for each idea.

The Five of Wands' traditional meanings of strife, difficulties, and competition are sound definitions, but the general message may not be deep enough if the card keeps reoccurring.

Five of Wands	Tarot Card Chosen	Response	Step of Action
First wand	Page of Cups	My son's choice of study for college	Find a good career counselor
Second wand	Two of Pentacles	Juggling too much	Create a better to-do system
Third wand	The Chariot	Need new front tires	Buy them
Fourth wand	King of Pentacles	Need an accountant	Ask my friend who she uses
Fifth wand	The Moon	Insomnia	No screens after 9 pm

The Five of Wands' steps of action form a strategy that goes beyond the traditional meanings. The result is a hand-tailored message with solutions

Up to this point of the book, the assumption is that the images of the cards are viewed in their upright positions. It is the reader's choice, however, to also read cards in a reversed position—that is, when the images appear upside down. Some readers never do. Tarot beginners could easily opt out, as there is enough information flowing through without the added pressure. Seasoned readers, however, may miss significant subtleties if they deny this additional layer of insight. Reversals may indicate a large reframing of a card, such as its opposite meaning, or indicate that something is absent. It may mean a subtlety, such as something you understand but others do not. An example: The Three of Swords in an upright position might mean deep sorrow or depression. Reversed, it may mean that healing has begun or a corner has been turned. Whether or not you choose to read reversals is one of the many choices you make as a reader.

Upright   Reversed

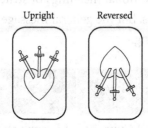

Three of Swords

Of your many reading preferences such as reading reversals or having the seeker shuffle the cards, the bones of the reading is the manner in which you lay the cards for interpretation. Spreads are the literal structure for the cards. Each position in a spread can be defined, for example, for a three-card spread you could define the three cards as body, mind, and spirit. Another option is to read the cards within a spread in a free-form manner much like reading a book, allowing one card to lead to the next. Story spreads are open structures that are readily used in either manner.

Story Spreads

Beginning readers may want to consider using simple spreads that provide an intuitive flow. As if you are reading a picture book, follow the meaning of one image to the next. Allow yourself to imagine a story unfolding rather than connecting the dots logically.

Three Card Spread

This spread provides an answer in the form of a story. You can read the cards using this spread by either defining the positions for each card or relying on a stream-of-consciousness flow. The three cards hold a wealth of possible assignments for positions, such as body-mind-spirit, you-me-us, or past-present-future, to name a few.

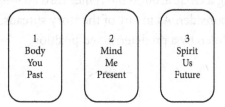

1	2	3
Body	Mind	Spirit
You	Me	Us
Past	Present	Future

Three Card Spread

Path Spread

This is an organic flow of three to seven cards. It is well-suited for any question in which a choice must be made, such as "Should I do this or should I do that?" The Path spread allows you to explore both. Choose three to seven cards for each path, laying them left to right, for each path signifies one option. It will give insights and possible outcomes of that particular choice. Gaining insight into each option will help the seeker be proactive. The different paths outline the likely ways each choice would be experienced.

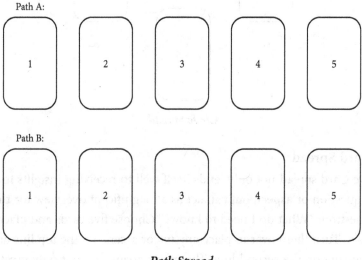

Path A:

| 1 | 2 | 3 | 4 | 5 |

Path B:

| 1 | 2 | 3 | 4 | 5 |

Path Spread

Circle Spread

The first card in the center represents the seeker or the question. The three to seven cards creating a circle around the center card are the various influences or perspectives to consider. As in any of the story spreads, a card can act as a free agent or be defined by a predetermined position.

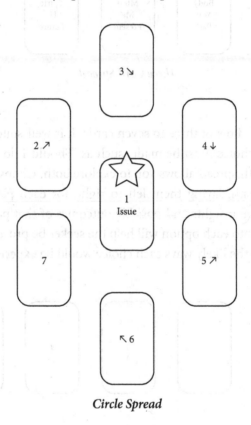

Circle Spread

Five Card Spread

The Five Card spread not only lends itself well to receiving insights to a particular question or aspect, but can act as a magnificent overview for the ultimate question: "What do I need to know?" Choose five cards and place them facedown. Turn them over to place any major arcana on the top line and any minor arcana on the second line. The major arcana are not only great influences, they also serve as energy storehouses of their essences. The minor arcana show how these major arcana play out in daily life.

If there are no major arcana, the solutions and dynamics of everyday life are all that are needed.

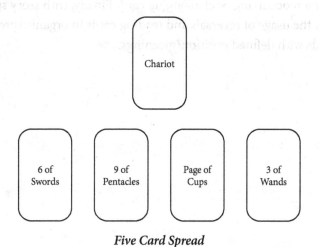

Five Card Spread

For example, the five cards chosen are the Six of Swords, Nine of Pentacles, the Chariot, Page of Cups, and Three of Wands. Place the Chariot on the top line with the others on the second line. The Chariot is a powerful influence offering resources of travel, momentum, aligning one's will, and motivation. The Six of Swords speaks to moving from turbulent times to calm ones. The Nine of Pentacles portrays a sense of purpose and feeling connected to your surroundings and work. The Page of Cups shows an opportunity of a new vision. The Three of Wands is an image that may portray waiting for desired manifestations. The Chariot acts as an engine in this context, keeping one's focus on doing what needs to be done as the progress, purpose, opportunity, and patience unfold in the seeker's life.

Summary

You are encouraged as a reader to create your own understanding of tarot through the rituals of Anointing the Deck and Entering the Card. The various tarot families each have their own ritual which can culminate into the Essence spread or stand alone. Exploring how the cards can reflect your life through the One Aspect ritual and the Card of the Day ritual creates confidence in your own perceptions. The Bears Repeating ritual is a creative analysis for a reoccurring or challenging card. Finally, with story spreads, we touched on the usage of reversals and reading cards in organic spreads rather than spreads with defined position/meanings.

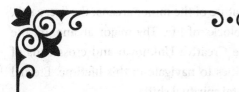

Chapter Four

THE MAJOR ARCANA

We have explored various ways to perceive magic by combining ritual and tarot. Hopefully you are giving yourself plenty of permission to flow with your curiosity and the imagery. Now, let us enter the big magic of the major arcana.

The major arcana are twenty-two portals to other dimensions of insight, power, and beauty. This chapter focuses on each of these power hitters. Change, add, and switch up the suggestions according to your inclinations.

Tarot offers a direct line to our Creative Unknown. This line varies for each practitioner. For some, it is a way to let wisdom flow more effectively by bypassing fear and ego. For others, it is a connection to a greater source of love for a bigger picture and greater clarity. No matter how you use the cards, trust your perceptions of the energy that travels through the imagery.

We have explored the elemental nature of the minor arcana: the fire, earth, water, and air seen as the building blocks of life. The major arcana, on the other hand, are different faces of the Creative Unknown and crossroads of change. They are potentials and realities to navigate in this lifetime. Eternal love pours through each of these pivotal spiritual shifts.

Before going further into the major arcana's blueprint, use the Entering the Card ritual (pg 25) to discover each of their essences. It helps to develop a personal understanding of these cards, especially if you are new to tarot.

Twenty-Two Acts Of Magic

The 22 Acts of Magic explores the magic of each of the major arcana. This template helps you step through each portal fully. Keep in mind that these are suggestions and not a definitive explanation of the major arcana. There are five components: the portal, the shadow, three modes in surfacing a true intention, crafting this intention, and the ritual. Depending on your focus and need, some of this work could take place over a few weeks or months. The intention is key for the desired alchemy. Please note that the pronoun "they" will be used in the guided journeys rather than specific gender designations. The five aspects of the template are:

1) The Portal
Key words and descriptions are given for each of the major arcana. These descriptors will hopefully give you a strong sense of each of their magical influences.

2) The Shadow
Issues, weaknesses, and symptoms are listed to reveal if you are experiencing the major arcana in its inverted power.

3) Preparation for the Ritual
All great magic is created by intent. Read all the suggestions and select those that pique your curiosity. Your own body sensations, writing prompts, and a guided visualization are the three creative ways to surface a necessary intention. For example, choosing the Empress major arcana, you become aware of the Empress's beautiful hair. You start to focus on your feelings and thoughts

about your own beauty. You decide to choose the writing prompt about a time you felt beautiful and connected. The journey really brings you in touch with an inner beauty. You craft an intention to reflect the beauty of love within and without.

A) FINDING THE INTENT—BODY WISDOM

The physical suggestions listed for embodiment can reveal your body's wisdom needed for a potent intent. Don't underestimate your body's ability to open new doors of perception. Insights such as images, messages, or sensations gathered as your body's response may be especially potent for readers with physical limitations.

B) FINDING THE INTENT—WRITING PROMPTS

The questions and writing prompts may trigger a hidden or neglected need necessary for effective magic. Let your curiosity guide the choice. A twenty-minute limit will prevent overthinking. Pulling cards randomly is suggested in all writing prompts. Pay special attention to any time the specific major arcana itself surfaces as a card. Synchronicity always speaks volumes in terms of mystery.

C) FINDING THE INTENT—JOURNEY

A guided visualization is a verbal walk-through of this major arcana. Recording the journey beforehand would be beneficial. The asterisk symbol * denotes taking a three-count pause (one Mississippi, two Mississippi, three Mississippi). Take some time after the visualization to sit with the various sensations and ideas that appeared.

4) Intention

The intention that surfaced in the preparation phase should clearly illustrate your desired manifestation. Any triggers, uneasiness, or lightbulb moments received during the preparation phase are clues to what is needed from that particular major arcana's portal. Suggestions will be given to help craft the intention if the body wisdom, writing prompts, and the journey did not surface anything significant.

5) Ritual Suggestion

Once you have a clear intention, you are ready for the ritual. Calling the Circle ritual (pg 17) will often be the suggested structure. All variations such as tarot selections, environment, and timing will enhance your experience of entering the portal. The outcome is to open to the Creative Unknown for new perceptions and realities. May all suggestions inspire better ideas of your own.

Let us begin!

The Fool Ritual

The Fool Portal

Without form or identity

Following one's instincts

Entering a new phase or territory

Actively being spirit-led

The Fool Shadow

Allowing others to determine the direction of your life

Stressed most of the time or easily

Impulsiveness leading to bad choices

Life feels mechanical

The Fool Preparation for the Ritual

FINDING THE INTENT—BODY WISDOM

Play with any physicality that changes gravity, e.g., swimming, floating, jumping, or being upside down.

Lead with your heart center as you move in an open space.

Stretch out your upper body.

Receive bodywork which makes you feel glad to be in your skin again.

Ask your body how it wants to move.

FINDING THE INTENT—WRITING PROMPTS

Randomly choose five to seven tarot cards to place in a circle (representing the Fool's numerical status of zero) for insights about what you need to gain from the Fool. Write about each message with new eyes. Don't go into any old stories.

Discover what surfaces with this set of declarative sentences:

"I don't know."

"I don't know who I am."

"I really don't know what is going on."

How is the Creative Unknown calling me?

What is worth the risk?

FINDING THE INTENT—JOURNEY

"I walk with an animal companion. They will alert me to any danger. I feel drawn forward as if someone is calling me. * The pressures of the world drop with each step that I take. I am free of linear time and concerns. * The path leads to a cliff overlooking an entire landscape. I stand still and look out. The feeling of gratefulness rises up within me. * My soul wants this body, this lifetime, the skills and gifts I have been given. * I am free of all patterns and beliefs. No story defines me as I follow my heart. * I carry a bag of the four soul tools: the sword, wand, cup, and pentacle. * I go toward the Creative Unknown calling me out into the sky of possibility."

The Fool Intention

What has surfaced as a major theme or need regarding The Fool? What healing might be needed? Take some time to craft a succinct statement. For example: "I lead a spirit-led life for myself and others."

The Fool Ritual Suggestion

Create a sense of risk and/or openness for this ritual. Go to a certain park or familiar landscape with a written version of the intention. Start with the Grounding ritual (page 12) or by simply calling in light through the crown of your head. Follow your curiosity within an hour's time. Go wherever you feel directed. Note all synchronicities such as anything you hear others say, nature, etc. When it feels right, read your intention out loud. Stay engaged with the natural world and others. Return to stand in the original spot of grounding. Thank all presences that have sent messages, visible and invisible.

Transform the received messages into those of a mythical quality at a later time. For instance, you overheard a person deep in conversation on their cell phone walking ahead of you. The tone felt intense and terse. A squirrel scampered suddenly in front of them which made them laugh out loud. The conversation afterward seemed to be lighter. The mythic message could be, "As I am spirit-led, interruptions can shift me into necessary delight."

The Magician Ritual

The Magician Portal
Manifesting one's true desire

Channeling divine energy

Creativity

Trusting one's own magic

The Magician Shadow
Inability to accomplish desired activity

Lacking will

Confusion about purpose

Life is predictable and rote

The Magician Preparation
FINDING THE INTENT—BODY WISDOM
Draw energy from the ground with each inhale.

Envision energy coming down through the crown of your head.

Explore forms, such as tai chi or Reiki, that view the body as energy.

Ask your body how it experiences the four elements of earth, air, water, and fire.

What is your greatest strength? Weakness?

What needs to be expressed through me?

How do I channel the Creative Unknown?

Choose a card for each of the four elements of the Essence spread (page 32). Describe a life-changing experience with each of the four elements.

FINDING THE INTENT—JOURNEY

"Trees provide a path for me. I go deeper into the forest. * As I walk, I am aware of the trees as brothers and sisters. * I see an altar in a circle of trees up ahead. This is my altar for my requests and awareness to serve love. * As I approach, I see that all four elements are represented on the altar. * I am a master of each within and without. * Air. * Fire. * Water. * Earth. * I take a stance to allow the power of creativity to fill me completely. * I am the bridge of the sky and the earth. I become the full potential of being both spirit and human."

The Magician Intention

Which part of the preparation phase was most inspiring? Assume that you are already an effective magician, what would you change in your life? This desired manifestation could be your intention.

The Magician Ritual Suggestion

Of all the major arcana, only the Magician uses an altar. Each of the four quarters could be their own altar. Separate the cards to place each suit in its direction—the swords in the east, the wands in the south, the cups in the west, and the pentacles in the north. Include symbols of that element such as a bowl of water in the west or perhaps a feather in the east.

Using Calling the Circle (pg 17), recite your intention out loud at each of the quarters. Visualize that elemental tool's gift in manifesting your desire. Choose one card randomly and place it faceup on top of its suit. After all four quarters have been opened and a card from their specific suit has been chosen, take your place in the center. Again, read your intention out loud. Open yourself to a spiral of silver light from the sky to come down through the crown of your head, as well as a spiral of green light that comes up through your feet from the earth. Bless the intention as you place both hands on your heart. Be in stillness. Sense the shift of energies. The four cards are a blueprint for the necessary energetic action or awareness.

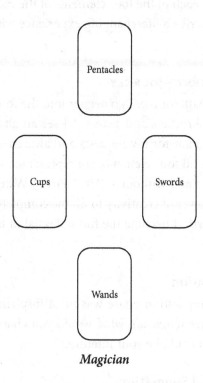

Magician

The High Priestess Ritual

The High Priestess Portal

Prophecy

Bear witness to others' secrets

Wisdom

Memory-keeper of the connection to source

The High Priestess Shadow

Over-responsible for others' well-being

Ineffective boundaries

Lost in illusion

Hearing but not listening to intuitive messages

The High Priestess Preparation

FINDING THE INTENT—BODY WISDOM

Sit, walk, or lie down as a meditative movement for at least fifteen minutes a day.

Use visualization to focus on chakras.

Move your torso, legs, and arms slowly and in waves, as if you are in an
ocean up to your thighs

Ask your body how it experiences your spirit.

FINDING THE INTENT—WRITING PROMPTS

Choose two cards randomly. One is for the High Priestess within and
the other for the scroll, the current mystery of your life. Write down
all triggers and memories being surfaced.

Imagine your favorite past-life training as a diviner.

What does the scroll say about your life currently and where it is being
directed?

Describe the mystery you have been tracking.

What secret do you guard?

FINDING THE INTENT—JOURNEY

"From wherever I stand, I can smell a salty tang of an ancient sea. * I pick
a direction to walk. Soon I spot a path. It leads to a desert of white sands. *
What I thought would be a great body of water is a simple and beautiful pool.
It seems to recognize and welcome me. * I stop and breathe. A temple slowly
starts to appear. * At first, I wonder if I am imagining this. As I wait and
watch, the temple form solidifies. * I enter. It takes a few minutes to adjust
to the darkness. * Eventually, I see a throne with two slender pillars on either
side of it. I feel beckoned to sit on the throne. I sit. * As I focus inward, I am
aware of centuries of wisdom flowing from the ancient sea that once covered
this desert. Its energies rise up through the throne. * I am able to remember

this planet at her beginnings. * I am firmly in the present moment. Peace washes through me. * I receive this flow with my entire being. I trust beyond my senses. I breathe fully."

The High Priestess Intention

The High Priestess is a beloved of most tarot folk. The path of the High Priestess, however, is a solitary one. All that is needed is from within. During the preparation, when did you feel like you were in the flow? Craft an intention that will give you confidence in holding your life as a holy scroll.

The High Priestess Ritual Suggestion

A new moon is a great launching time to create magic. This is especially true for the High Priestess. With intention clearly stated, write it on a scroll and roll it up. Use Calling the Circle (pg 17). Honor the four quarters and the center with candles. Sit in the center with the scroll and tarot cards. This would be an ideal time to initiate a new or unused deck, crystals, and other tools.

The highlight of this ritual is a five-card spread. Choose each card for insight as a direct response to your intention. You can read the cards this way:

1. *Essence:* This card represents the essence of your intention.

2 and 3. *Pillars:* These two cards represent the two pillars. These are two beliefs that are powerful influences regarding the intention. Put judgments aside and observe what is being truly depicted.

4. *Resistance:* This card portrays what is preventing clear sight. In what ways are you unable to access your own wisdom about this intention? What is necessary to be fully present?

5. *Mystery:* The final card represents the mystery of your intention. Receive this. Dream on this card. Allow its insights to unfold slowly. Consider creating a high priestess altar that displays this card alone until the next moon cycle.

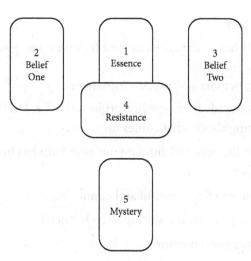

High Priestess

The Empress Ritual

The Empress Portal

Abundance

Gestating creations

Mother Nature

Unconditional love

The Empress Shadow

Rejecting deep feelings

Reactive instead of responsive

Self-negligence

Disconnected from the body's natural rhythms

The Empress Preparation

FINDING THE INTENT—BODY WISDOM

Focus on self-care such as a soak in a tub, receiving bodywork, or a pedicure.

Take time to stretch out kinks.

Change your hair.

Ask your body how it experiences your feminine energies.

FINDING THE INTENT—WRITING PROMPTS

Pull three tarot cards for a new life, project, or idea. Don't be rational when writing about what comes up.

Describe how different and similar your own path has been with that of your mother.

Write of a time you felt beautiful and connected.

Which creative projects are waiting to be birthed?

Who has been a good mentor?

FINDING THE INTENT—JOURNEY

"I go to an open space within a landscape I love. * No one else is here except for wildlife. I feel connected and loved. * Above me is the sun or the moon and stars. A light beams down through my whole being. I connect to the ground. * I am part of nature. I feel all the weather within me, the rain, the lightning, and the snow. * Within my being are universes waiting to be born. I feel their vitality with grace. * I am loved. I love."

The Empress Intention

Base your intention on your heart's desire. Listening to your true nature, what would benefit your life most? What is needed for this current cycle?

The Empress Ritual Suggestion

Plan time outdoors or at least away from your day-to-day life for this ritual. Once there, travel with your cards in nature. In silence, hold your intention loosely as if you were airing it out. Stop moving when you sense the perfect spot. Speak your intention out loud three times. Pull three cards as responses. Stay aware of any messages coming from the nature around you. Slowly look at each card. Feel the roots underneath you stir. Envision the intention change with each of the three responses. Leave something as a gift at this spot before thanking any loving presence that contributed.

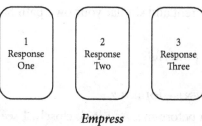

Empress

The Emperor Ritual

The Emperor Portal

Structure

Rules of society

Effective strategy

Owning one's true power

The Emperor Shadow

Highly disorganized

Ineffective leadership

Hard time delegating

Avoiding responsibility

The Emperor Preparation

FINDING THE INTENT—BODY WISDOM

Build up your vitality and endurance with weight lifting, climbing stairs, using an elliptical machine regularly, or another strength-building exercise of your choice. It is wise to check with a medical provider before beginning an exercise program. Do simple core-strengthening exercises daily.

Ask your body how it experiences your masculine energies.

FINDING THE INTENT—WRITING PROMPTS

Choose four cards. Write about the strategy you have for your life going forward, implementing the messages from these cards.

What is a long-game strategy for your life?

Define your present personal power.

Describe how different and similar your own path has been with that of
your father.

When do you feel powerful?

Finding the Intent—Journey

"I see a mountain before me. As I look closely, I see many stone steps. *
I start to climb. * Along the way, I see small and intricate shrines. * I start
to feel the climb. My heart is beating faster. I enjoy feeling the power in my
limbs. * The view takes my breath away at times. Eventually I am among the
treetops. I can sense a low hum from the mountain itself. * When I am about
ready to give up from the exertion, I enter a shrine grander than any of the
others along the way. The air is electric. There is a great throne. * I want to
sit on this throne. As I sit, I feel the rush of my full power. It takes a while to
adjust to this shift. I am alive and clear. * I can see my life flow powerfully
from this vista."

The Emperor Intention

Carefully pay attention to messages regarding power. The intention could be
based on clarity, strategy, or taking up one's full authority.

The Emperor Ritual Suggestion

Create a ritual as if the intention has been fully manifested. Rather than it
being a journey to the top of the mountain, act as if you are looking back at
the starting point. Imagine it from that angle of accomplishment. Use Calling the Circle (pg 17) to open the quarters. Settle in the center and imagine
being in the full power of the intention. Read it out loud. Channel this intention as your future self. Consciously choose two or three cards as reminders
of this message. Use the cards as building blocks of your desired intention.

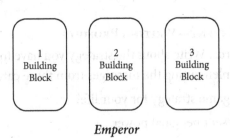

Emperor

The Hierophant Ritual

The Hierophant Portal

Lineage

Teacher

Rituals

Sacred templates

The Hierophant Shadow

Being overly extravagant

Unconnected to source

Life feels meaningless

Absence of any spiritual practice

The Hierophant Preparation

FINDING THE INTENT—BODY WISDOM

Explore a practice of great lineage such as tai chi, yoga, or belly dancing.

Do a sequence of movements designed to release stress, such as the Six
Healing Sounds of Taoism, to start or end the day.

Ask your body what gestures it considers to be powerful.

FINDING THE INTENT—WRITING PROMPTS

Choose five cards. Base a story on your spiritual evolution using these
cards.

Whom do you serve?

How do you connect to sacred energy on a regular basis?

Which traditions from childhood have nurtured you? Harmed you?

Who or what is holy?

FINDING THE INTENT—JOURNEY

"As I stand, I am slowly enveloped by a mist. It feels warm and has a slight
smell of incense. * It completely covers me until I can no longer see. * I am
being moved within this mist. Eventually I sense a landing as the mist slowly

descends around my feet. I have been transported to a specific lifetime under a great spiritual teacher. * I remember living here in a strong, simple fashion. I knew what was expected of me. I knew who and what I served with my whole life. * I go to a scene of a loving community. * The teacher recognizes my current presence! * They ask me how I have grown since we were together. * We communicate with each other on many levels. * They bless my current efforts to surface valuable core lessons. * I return to my current life feeling seen, supported, and sacred."

The Hierophant Intention

Note anything that was surprising during the preparation phase. Of all the major arcana, the Hierophant's intention can be one for a spirit-led life, spiritual practice, or effective techniques.

The Hierophant Ritual Suggestion

This ritual is effective with all the props, sounds, and incense. List any religious or spiritual aspects of your experience that have fed your soul, such as the music, the stained glass windows, chanting, or prayers. Choose ones to honor the Hierophant within. Let these preferences enhance Calling the Circle (pg 17). Create a sacred space with a central altar table. Have all the elements represented with a specific color candle: east-yellow, south–red, west–blue, north–green, and center–white. Plan any gestures and soundtrack that will enhance the intention. Allow the height of the ceremony to be breath or meditation in silence. Receive the messages, insights, or energy of your intention. Ask for a blessing from each of the quarters as you face that direction and choose one tarot card.

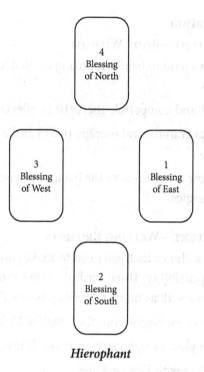

Hierophant

The Lovers Ritual

The Lovers Portal

Making authentic choices

Collaboration

Dialogue of heart and mind

Integration of one's masculinity and femininity

The Lovers Shadow

Attract toxic relationships

Emotionally or mentally overwhelmed

Unable to take action

Judgmental

The Lovers Preparation

FINDING THE INTENT—BODY WISDOM

Most of our bodies tend to be either strong or pliable—develop your weaker aspect.

Find a competent and compatible therapist to alleviate chronic patterns.

Modalities such as craniosacral therapy (CST) and acupuncture are powerful forms.

Ask your body how it experiences the balance of your feminine and masculine energies.

FINDING THE INTENT—WRITING PROMPTS

Pull six cards for a choice that you need to make soon. Three of the cards describe one possibility. Three cards describe another option. Write about each path with as much neutrality as possible.

How do you receive messages from the Creative Unknown?

Do you tend to neglect or oppress your masculine or feminine aspects?

Speak to encounters with Divine Allies.

FINDING THE INTENT—JOURNEY

"I stand at a familiar crossroad. It seems as if I have been here before. * I desire to be more real and authentic. I close my eyes to hear what my heart desires at this time in my life. * When I open my eyes, I see three roads. One goes left, one straight ahead, and the other goes right. * Each of these roads will lead me to a desired destination. Only their length and processes vary. * It is important that I choose the process as well as the destination. * One road will require change and much patience. * Another road brings mystery and surprises that could possibly change the destination. I would need to trust each step because I will not be able to see ahead. * The third road is a continuation of where I stand now with my current choices. This road will undoubtedly lead me to a similar crossroad ahead. * Without judgment, I take my first step onto the road I need now. There is no going back."

The Lovers Intention

What would your intention be if you were free of habitual thinking and feeling? How is the Creative Unknown nudging you? Trust the observer and the feeler within to trust a greater vision of your life.

The Lovers Ritual Suggestion

Create three altars to represent the masculine, feminine, and spirit of The Lovers card. See yourself in all of its components. Identify the masculine symbology as the world. It is what is manifested and acknowledged by others. It is work, thought, and action. The feminine is earth—our being, body, connection, and creations. The spirit is sacredness, time without time, guidance, and wisdom. When ready, open sacred space through Calling the Circle (pg 17). Randomly choose one card at each station. Be guided by your Divine Allies and Beloved Ancestors. Go to the center. Envision all three aspects merging seamlessly into a spiral of light around you.

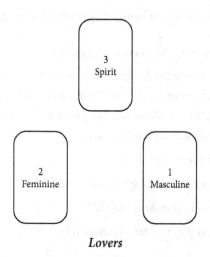

Lovers

The Chariot Ritual

The Chariot Portal

Aligning the personal will with the divine will

Managing ego with presence

Mastering your emotions and thoughts

Confidence in personal strengths and management of weaknesses

The Chariot Shadow

Easily distracted

Willpower alone is not effective

Things seem out of control

Little movement or progression

The Chariot Preparation

FINDING THE INTENT—BODY WISDOM

Use your non-dominant hand in regular tasks.

Occasionally don't wear your glasses in your living space.

Develop balance exercises.

Seek professional feedback about your body's overall structure, your
   strengths, weaknesses, et cetera. This could include muscle testing,
   acupuncture, bodywork that includes stretching, or a personal trainer.

Ask your body to show you how it experiences strength and weakness.

FINDING THE INTENT—WRITING PROMPTS

Pull seven cards. Three cards are your strengths, three will be your
   weaknesses. The remaining card is your chariot—your body, will,
   or personality. Write about the big picture here in terms of your
   motivation and movement forward.

What needs your focus and drive?

How do you procrastinate or get distracted?

Which goals seem unattainable lately?

Where or when do you not trust yourself?

FINDING THE INTENT—JOURNEY

"I stand feeling more myself than ever. I envision my inherent set of skills
and traits that serve others and myself well. * With each breath, I open myself
to presence and love within. * I now call to mind times of fear and my reac-
tions then. * These default patterns have at times oppressed myself and oth-

ers. * I feel a surge of determination to move beyond past conditioning. * I move forward with a better understanding of myself. * I release being wrong or right. There is no need to push. I move forward in support and trust."

The Chariot Intention

Hopefully through the preparation phase, an issue or desire surfaced calling for Chariot magic. Select an aspect in your life that could use better flow and focus.

The Chariot Ritual Suggestion

Plan a road trip. Have a general idea of a destination but remain open to synchronicity and messages. Throughout the entire trip, do only one thing at a time. For example, if driving, do not listen to the radio. If eating, don't read. With an open road and no distraction, note all the discomfort that may arise. Make your way to a spot and set up Calling the Circle (pg 17). Read the intention aloud. Choose one card for the strength and one for the weakness inherent in the intention. Listen. Go within. Allow the Creative Unknown to become the driver.

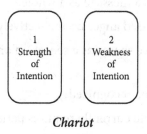

Chariot

Strength Ritual

Strength Portal

Confronting feelings long hidden from conscious thought

Honoring all feelings

Nonreactive responses

Liberate passion from fear

Strength Shadow

Unduly hard on yourself and others

Neglect your own needs

Impatience

Overwhelmed by desires, fears, or confusion

Strength Preparation

FINDING THE INTENT—BODY WISDOM

Define small steps that would change your relationship with your body.
Examples could be getting to bed a half hour earlier, not eating after
6 p.m., and moving in some way, shape, or form daily.

Allow a unique understanding of your sexuality and sensuality to arise.

Ask your body what needs your support and compassion.

FINDING THE INTENT—WRITING PROMPTS

Choose eight cards. Each will contribute to a larger message of managing
your needs under all circumstances. Write instant ideas or triggers for
each card and then a message as a whole.

When have you witnessed anger used effectively?

How do you experience shame as a sensation or feeling? What can trigger it?

What desires need to be recognized?

What sphere of your life currently requires patience and care?

FINDING THE INTENT—JOURNEY

"I stand at the brink of a wild terrain. * As I breathe, I feel long and loose.
* I am about to enter a territory of various influences on my psyche, ego,
and my old conditioning. I may encounter the shame learned instead of love
needed. Before stepping forward, I consider what these aspects might be. * I
am safe and protected as I move slowly forward. * This is a wild space. I feel

sensual, as if I am moving about as a giant cat. * In the distance, I sense a disturbance. Older sensations and fears start to swell in my heart. I decide to keep going. * I come upon a spiral of dark colors. As I watch it spin in place, I am aware of the deepest parts of myself that I have always hated. * Rather than letting it continue, I ask for the spiral to transform into an animal. I will meet this animal, my beast, with full power and love. It is a part of me that appears to be separate from my heart. * It charges me. I breathe and let love flow through me. * My bare hands catch the beast. It cannot do any harm. The force of love settles it down. * The illusion of separateness dissipates. * I remain calm. It is becoming an experience within myself. The splintered isolations from self-hate dissolve. * I watch as the animal merges into a spiral of a vital light."

Strength Intention

Self-acceptance will require compassion and patience. What is needed to bring a greater sense of peace and wholeness to your life? State an intention of love overcoming fear, shame, regret, or unworthiness.

Strength Ritual Suggestion

Using Calling the Circle, speak your intention out loud eight times once in center. Be aware of any fear or doubts that arise. Consider how your life may proceed if this intention doesn't surface. Let your ego have at it! Your inner cynic or old conditioning may shoot holes through the intention. Stay calm yet engaged with any doubts.

Fear not only resides in the mind and heart, it also has stationed itself in your body. Speak the fears aloud and sense how your body responds. Put your hands on those areas as you envision a healing beam of light. Take all the time necessary for the light to disperse the fear or tightness. Afterward, fill with compassion. Do a Circle spread (page 38) for instructions in growing this new presence.

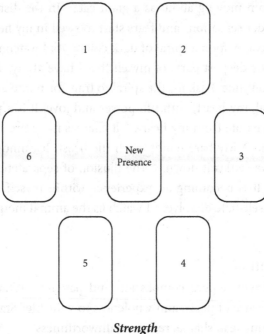

Strength

The Hermit Ritual

The Hermit Portal

Listening to self and spirit

Developing and maintaining a vital spiritual practice

Healthy separation from worldly concerns

The Hermit Shadow

You are isolated without connection

Can't find peace of mind

Too busy

The Hermit Preparation

FINDING THE INTENT—BODY WISDOM

Move to music allowing your body to move freely.

Find a form that allows the body to speak. Move following the body's impulses.

Modalities such as Authentic Movement, contact improvisation, and InterPlay liberate your body's innate wisdom.

Ask your body to show you how it enjoys stillness.

FINDING THE INTENT—WRITING PROMPTS

Look through your tarot deck to mindfully choose all cards that have a specific light source. This could be literal light such as the Sun card or a card that evokes a sense of light, like the Nine of Pentacles. Write about the power of light in your life from these cards' messages.

Describe the last time you heard silence.

What helps quiet your mind? Your being?

Speak of the person who held a light for you during a time of crisis.

How are you different when alone?

FINDING THE INTENT—JOURNEY

"I stand surrounded in nature. I am alone yet I am only one of many beings under this starry night. * I share this space with animals, birds, trees, plants, and stone. * I honor all of my teachers and teachings that have led me to this moment. * Like a Star, I am part of a constellation, shining with others. I belong here. * My wisdom is flowing and full. My ability to hear my own truth is effortless. * My own light helps me navigate through the dark. I lift the lamp up to see further. * Those that need my light notice more in their lives. * I become aware of many other lights. We are separated but connected, single yet whole together."

The Hermit Intention

Within a meditation, gather the various ideas, needs, and concerns raised during the preparation phase to craft them into an intention. A long soak in the tub, an uninterrupted walk in silence, or simply sitting quietly for fifteen minutes may allow a significant need to surface. Stay engaged but unattached to the outcome.

The Hermit Suggested Ritual

The ritual is done in seclusion over the span of a few days to honor your intention. If possible, schedule a desert night retreat—a full day between two nights. This private space (or disconnecting at home) is a deliberate opening to the Creative Unknown. The first night involves rest and leaving all connection to the outside world—screens, phones, other folks. The day is an active immersion of mindfully holding your intention. Stay open to the flow of messages around you. Note any synchronicities with nature, ideas, or dreams received while in this quiet state of being and listening. If you are within the vicinity of others, what messages might you overhear? How do they relate to your intention?

When ready, open the basic ceremony in the late afternoon or evening. Speak your intention out loud. Meditate in this sacred space for at least fifteen minutes. Read aloud the gathered messages and activities. Choose three cards for the Creative Unknown's response to your intention. After you close the circle, spend your remaining time in gratitude.

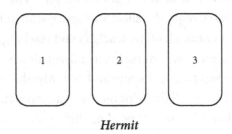

Hermit

The Wheel of Fortune Ritual

The Wheel of Fortune Portal

Significant changes

Releasing attachments

Karma

The Wheel of Fortune Shadow

Overly attached to desired outcomes

Remain passive or resistant to necessary changes

Lost connection to the seasons

The Wheel of Fortune Preparation

FINDING THE INTENT—BODY WISDOM

Find a body movement or method that orients your whole being in the present moment. Examples are a deep nap, floating in water, or the dead man's pose after a yoga sequence. These physical experiences can transform changes and stress with time and ease.

Ask your body about its perspectives of the changes it has gone through.

FINDING THE INTENT—WRITING PROMPTS

Pull five tarot cards, one for each of the four seasons and the other representing a specific project/focus. Write about the progression of this project starting with the next season of the ritual.

What or who are you holding onto? What is holding onto you?

Describe any change that felt like a major detour at the time.

What is changing?

Describe your understanding of the purpose for this incarnation.

FINDING THE INTENT—JOURNEY

"I stand in a wild terrain. I can see all around me and above me for miles. Gray, stormy clouds start to appear. I feel the chill of a storm brewing. * Flashes and streaks of lightning start to light up the sky. * I am aware that I am in the open. I should fear for my safety but do not. * In the glimpses of white light, a prophet of this land approaches me. I now understand why I feel no fear. * They lead me to a better position to view a firework of lightning. * A big, fiery wheel appears in the sky. It is a great mandala, a spinning wheel of patterns and symbols. * I am being shown a form of the universe's rhythms. All outer forms seem to vanish. * I observe this great image as an underlying order of all of life. It is the wheel of time and space. * I feel free of all desires and needs. I sense no separation. I am with what is."

The Wheel of Fortune Intention

The Wheel of Fortune's magic is that of change. What did you discover as a necessary one? Write the intention in present time as if the desired change has happened. Describe the result and the way it makes you feel.

The Wheel of Fortune Ritual Suggestion

The Rider-Waite-Smith Wheel of Fortune image contains many powerful symbols—a sphinx, a king, a grasping hand, and four biblical evangelists. Use these mysterious figures as visual energies if you like. They dance in a wheel of time that holds the center of timelessness.

Designate the time preference for your intention's manifestation—for example, within fourteen days, three seasons, or two years. Using Calling the Circle, designate each quarter as a road post of the intention's timeline. Begin with the east. For example, if you would like the intention to manifest within a year, the east could be spring. Create a strong, visual energy of the intention becoming reality over time. Begin the ritual by lighting candles and opening the quarters. Once the sacred space has been created, slowly walk three times among the four quarters before taking your place in the center. The center is the seat of insight. Have your deck facedown in a circle around the seat. Take some time to settle into your breath. Let all outer reality dissipate. Say the intention out loud to your Divine Allies and Beloved Ancestors. Invite a vision to come to you. A timer or soundtrack might help with being fully receptive.

Let your hand scan the circle of cards in a clockwise motion. You may feel a pull to a certain section. Pull one or two cards to indicate your current reality.

Now scan the circle counterclockwise. Again, you will feel pulled to a certain section. Pull a few cards that reflect your resistance.

Finally, find one card in the circle that is your center. Choose one that feels full and rich. This image or message will help you stay strong during the change.

Allow your instant sense of the messages. Contemplate these cards. When done, reverse your steps to enter "real time" in gratitude of all loving presence during the ritual.

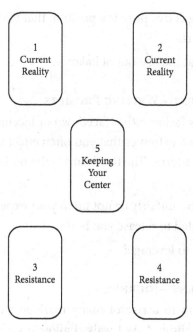

Wheel of Fortune

Justice Ritual

Justice Portal

Leveraging correctly

Speaking your truth

Spiritual laws and consequences

Justice Shadow

Dishonesty with yourself and others

Critical and judgmental

Self-neglect

Justice Preparation

FINDING THE INTENT—BODY WISDOM

Heart chakra exercises would be beneficial.

Find ways to explore balance and leverage with your own body weight.

Try vacuuming or carrying a load of groceries done in a more supported way. Yoga's tree pose is a position that will challenge habitual physical patterns.

Ask your body what may be out of balance.

FINDING THE INTENT—WRITING PROMPTS

Choose three cards (select either facedown or faceup). Two of the cards represent the two extremes that you often enact when acting from your habitual patterns. The third card is the middle path, a current response.

Who has treated you unfairly or not up to your expectations? What forgiveness is needed to release you both?

What do you need to leverage?

FINDING THE INTENT—JOURNEY

"I stand looking up to a rise of many marbled steps. I cannot see the destination. I start to climb. * As I walk, I allow myself to fully think about injustices that I have experienced. I recall those involved. I remember how it affected me. * I continue walking up the many stairs. There is an open, bright sky all around. It almost feels as if it is illuminated by fire. * I start to think of those that I hurt directly and inadvertently. I can hear my own rationalizations. I sense the bigger picture that has occurred since then. * I reach the top of the stairs. I can now see Justice seated on their throne. They are blindfolded, holding a sword in one hand and a scale in the other. * They move the scale toward me. * On one end of the scale, I am to place a great wish for my life. * On the other end of the scale I place the injustices, detours, and wrongs committed by myself and others. * I stand back in silence. We wait for love to balance the scale. I help by sending forgiveness. * I am in the presence of cosmic law. Much of this I may never understand. My letting go of all these past hurts is now being leveraged by love. * My heart lightens. * Justice pulls back the scale. I sense a smile. I thank them as I start my departure. * I return with a lighter heart."

Justice Intention

Note any insights or "aha" moments gathered from the preparatory explorations. Which stirred your heart? Which would feed your heart if transformed? Listen to your truths to create the intention most needed.

Justice Ritual Suggestion

As you open the quarters, call out a request for peace to the northern, southern, eastern, and western lands. Claim an outer circle of justice for all beings. Go to the center to have your truth balanced by the force of love. Speak your intention. Allow the scales to work as mentioned in the journey meditation. Love will eventually balance all. Choose three cards as images of wisdom. Press each one onto your heart before receiving its message.

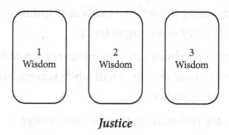

Justice

The Hanged Man Ritual

The Hanged Man Portal

    New perspectives

    Suspension

    Surrender

    Withdrawal from society

The Hanged Man Shadow

    Self-denial or neglect

    Seeking approval from others

    Refusing change or guidance

The Hanged Man Preparation

FINDING THE INTENT—BODY WISDOM

Take on physical positions or stretches that help you see things differently.

Perhaps you could lie outside to look at a night sky, float on water, or
do a head or shoulder stand. Remain in a stretch comfortably for
a length of time.

Wear colored sunglasses.

Ask your body how it wants to be viewed by you.

FINDING THE INTENT—WRITING PROMPTS

Shuffle your deck to make certain that some cards will be reversed.
Choose three. Write about the ways you are starting to perceive
life differently using these three cards as inspiration. In this spread,
reversed cards carry more importance.

Explore the ways you submit rather than surrender. Submitting is negat-
ing the power of your own free will while surrendering is entering a
state of true vulnerability.

How/what/who are you starting to view differently?

FINDING THE INTENT—JOURNEY

"I am surrounded by a canopy of trees. * I hear birds and feel a mild breeze
through the leaves. * Nearby I hear the sound of a creek. I walk toward it. * I
walk along the creek knowing that somewhere within this forest is the tree
of life. It has deep roots in the underworld. Its trunk is in this world while its
branches cover the upper world. * The creek leads to a large pool of emerald
water. It sits directly in front of the tree of life. I am in awe of this majestic tree.
* I gaze into the water. I see a being with a glowing face look back at me. They
magically hang from one foot to a huge branch of the tree of life. * Their eyes
are splendid. There is a gold aura all around their body. * I am not here to free
them. They need no help since they are connected to a powerful source and
are deep within their own freedom. * I sit by the pond and allow myself to
want nothing. * After some time has passed, I quietly stand, give thanks, and
start my return. I trust my thoughts and perceptions. I know what is true of
my reality."

The Hanged Man Intention

A full sense of being in the present moment is challenging in a culture of speed and convenience. Slow down. Take the time needed to create an intention that brings a sense of holiness—wholeness.

The Hanged Man Ritual Suggestion

Separate the suits and place them facedown in the four quarters according to Calling the Circle. To open the ritual, go to each direction (starting with east) and randomly choose one tarot card. This card speaks of what is needed to be surrendered for the intention to manifest. The east is the thought pattern, the south speaks to the desire, the west shows the emotional belief, and the north speaks to the needed resources.

Create a ritualistic sacrifice for the center meditation. Examples: burning a list of your interpretation of the four chosen cards, sending off a paper boat or floating flowers in a river, or using flying wish paper. Burying a crystal or stone imbued with your intent near a favorite tree is highly recommended.

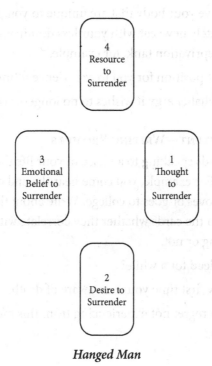

Hanged Man

Death Ritual

Death Portal

Transformation

Change of form

Death of the old self

Endings

Death Shadow

Boredom

Stuck in old habits

Can't or won't let go of things that you no longer need

Death Preparation

FINDING THE INTENT—BODY WISDOM

Explore movement without the attachment of exercise.

Find ways to move your body that are unique to you. Experience something completely new: eat with your less dominant hand, or float in an sensory deprivation tank, for example.

Discover the best position for you to experience ultimate stillness.

Ask your body what energy it wishes to no longer carry.

FINDING THE INTENT—WRITING PROMPTS

Choose three cards speaking to a phase in your life that is done or near completion. For example, you come near the end of parenting when your child moves or goes to college. Write about the perceptions received from the cards whether they correlate with your own current understanding or not.

What has been dead for a while?

Speak to the very first time you were aware of death.

What would you regret not experiencing from this moment to the time of your death?

FINDING THE INTENT—JOURNEY

"I stand in a barren field. The sun has started to set. The sky glows red. The wind and crows create a soundscape. * I can hear my footsteps as I walk through the field. There is no path. * A horse without a rider appears to my left. * After we make eye contact, the horse turns. I follow. * In the distance I see a skeleton who is harvesting with a huge scythe. They cut wheat with mighty swings. * I continue to walk alongside the horse. We are silent companions. * I see a figure of someone standing by a huge tree. I am aware that they are spirit. * As I come near to them, the horse wanders off. I recognize this spirit as myself. This is no other than my future self, the one before the day of my death. * They are as curious to see me as well. They show me a vision of what I could experience if I was fearless. * I thank them. I turn back to walk. * Lines of people that I have loved and that have passed form two columns. I walk between them and receive their blessings. * I return to where I appeared for this journey. I am blessed."

Death Intention

Birth to death is a common rhythm. Consider however going from death to birth. This major arcana isn't called "Dying," it is the Death card. What needs to be buried properly? You might base your intention on any aspect that would strengthen your resolve to fully live.

Death Ritual Suggestion

Do some preliminary research about different death rites. Fictional rituals are applicable. What grabs your imagination? Base your ritual as a variation of any rite that resonates strongly as a crossing-over ceremony.

What part of you needs a proper burial? Create a cut-out figure of a person to act as a placeholder of sorts. Read your intention as you hold your hand over the paper figure to bless this part of you that needs released. When ready, burn or bury this symbolic stand in. This ritual actively clears the space needed for growth. Choose five cards. Place them in any order you wish. From these cards, create a blessing for what needed to be released.

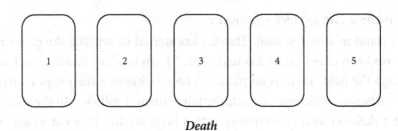

Death

Temperance Ritual

Temperance Portal

Grace

Alchemy

Angelic guardians

Recovery

Temperance Shadow

Jumping from one extreme to another

Disconnected from a natural flow

Lack of trust that things will change and/or improve

Temperance Preparation

FINDING THE INTENT—BODY WISDOM

Take a walk that falls between a slow saunter and a jog. Maintain this middle pace as long as possible before slowing down.

Consider physical moves that strengthen overall coordination and improve a sense of flow through your spine. A Pilates video, inversion table, or neck cradle may do the trick.

Ask your body how it flows.

FINDING THE INTENT—WRITING PROMPTS

Pull two cards focusing on two spheres of your life that could better support each other. Example: work and home life. Each card represents one of the spheres.

What can you imagine would be the way to bridge them better?

Describe moments during a crisis when you unexpectedly experienced calm and grace.

What is your divine nature?

FINDING THE INTENT—JOURNEY

"I stand on a path. It leads toward two rounded hills in the distance. The sun beams brightly. * As I walk, my heartbeat quickens. I sense different energy as I approach the hills. * I walk between these two hills. An entire valley opens in front of me. It is full of flowers. A few huge birds are soaring gracefully. * A pond glistens in the sunlight. As I get closer, one of the birds descends. I realize it isn't a bird but an angelic being. * It feels as if we had arranged to meet here. They move differently than I had imagined. * We understand and respond to one another although I can barely breathe in this being's presence. * There are two cups perched near the pond. We each pick up one cup. * We fill our cups from the pond and drink. * A shift within starts to happen. My own identity merges into something far bigger and spacious. * The angel reaches for my cup. It floats to them. With both cups, they hover above the pond and blend the waters of both cups. * I feel another shift within. My divine nature intertwines with my human self. * The angel flies high above into a distant rainbow."

Temperance Intention

An intention to feel the support of a Divine Ally is a powerful one. Carefully consider what needs more grace, mindfulness, and moderation in your life. Angels come to our assistance if invited.

Temperance Ritual Suggestion

Bring two cups to a body of water or close to an angelic statue in a cemetery. Record your intention on paper so that it can lie on top of both cups. Meditate and ask for a Divine Ally to hear this intention. Ask for angelic guidance. Use the Power of Pretend if needed; an angel will hear you. Cut the intention in half and place a part in each cup. Sense a feeling that may then descend all around you. Choose one tarot card that will act as a bridge for these two cups. Lift both cups and imagine a flow between them. Keep these two cups with their halves of the intention on your altar or somewhere within daily view for two weeks. Interpret the chosen card as a message of the alchemy needed to manifest the intention.

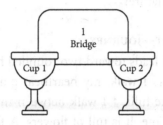

Temperence

The Devil Ritual

The Devil Portal

Ego

Materialism

Falsehoods

Obsession/addiction

The Devil Shadow

Detachment from needs and desires

Apathy regarding consequences

Self-judgment

The Devil Preparation

FINDING THE INTENT—BODY WISDOM

Indulge yourself with mindfulness and deliberation.

Get a physical for true data about weight, cholesterol, etc.

Purge all clothes or accessories that no longer work.

Ask your body to show you how to be responsibly irresponsible.

FINDING THE INTENT—WRITING PROMPTS

Pull three tarot cards. The first card represents light. The second is
    shadow. The third card speaks of the dark. Interpret these titles in any
    way you see fit. Are they applicable to your life currently?

List all the pretty lies you want to hear, and from whom you'd like to hear them.

What do you hide from others? From yourself?

FINDING THE INTENT—JOURNEY

"I stand looking up to a dark temple. Fifteen steps lead to its entry. I start the walk. * At the front entrance, the door opens as if on cue. I enter the temple. * Just a few feet inside, old fears and insecurities start to build within me. I start to feel disoriented in time. It increases with each step. * I am determined to face my past ghosts. I search for the room that seems as heavy as my heart in this moment. * I enter the room. A solitary mirror stands in the center. I approach it carefully. * When I stand inches from it, an image of myself appears. This image haunts me. It reflects a likeness of myself in crystal perfection. They have the body I have always wanted, are in full control of themselves and need no one. I look into the eyes of this self. I start to recognize the lies, ego, and expectations of others. * It is my ego fully visible. I cannot destroy it but am moved to destroy the mirror. A tool suited for this job appears. * I relish the destruction of self-denigration and insecurities spent in this life of never being enough. * I shatter the mirror. As the image splinters, the pain of shame and burden lift. * I no longer sense the tormenting pain within. My light starts to grow immediately. I stand very still as my light expands beyond my body to this room, the hallway, and then the entire temple. * Liberation is mine. I leave the temple."

The Devil Intention

Craft an intention based on fearlessness and fullness. Which desires and wishes need recognition? What choice would you really want to make right now?

The Devil Ritual Suggestion

Consider a strong limiting belief that may have surfaced through the preparation. Consciously choose any tarot cards that contain the energy of that fear or illusion. Using Calling the Circle, prepare the center by creating a circle of these chosen cards. Once seated, pick up the cards one by one. Locate the energy of the first card in your body. Imagine you can pull that energy out of your body. Act as if you can transfer that energy into both hands. Once it is pulled out completely, rub your hands furiously to transform the energy. Slowly open your hands to see the spirit's response of a new symbol, light, or image to replace that space. Hold your hands over the spot and imagine the new energy to replace the toxic pattern. Repeat this with each chosen card. When finished, read your intention aloud from a more fully embodied presence.

The Tower Ritual

The Tower Portal

Abrupt and large changes

Flash of enlightenment

Transformation of falsehoods and outgrown modes of being

The Tower Shadow

Easily defeated by challenges

Constantly choosing comfort over growth

Avoiding conflict at all costs

The Tower Preparation

FINDING THE INTENT—BODY WISDOM

Find a therapist to assist in somatic release of trauma.

Learn body tapping.

Go on a long walk to nowhere to let the body carry the mind.

Ask your body if it would show you how it is healing.

FINDING THE INTENT—WRITING PROMPTS

Pull three cards. The first represents the tower—an old coping skill. The second is the lightning bolt—the change needed to strike down all that keeps you from love. The third card represents the falling persons—leaving this self-made prison. Describe the ways you have learned to cope. How have any of these become a prison rather than a sanctuary? What unwanted dynamic seems to repeat over and over? What red flags are you avoiding?

FINDING THE INTENT—JOURNEY

"I stand looking into the distance at a large gray tower. * I built this tower brick by brick over the years as a way to be safe. I walk slowly toward it. * As I enter the tower, I am aware of the many rooms holding old memories. They constantly loop as movies. These are all the scenes of times when I felt I was not worth love. I wasn't safe to be me. * There is a long winding staircase that passes by all the rooms. I can choose to look into each room or proceed to the top floor. * I feel the shame and fear all around me. I keep going. I realize that the source of these scenes is the pain from others. * I reach the top. There are three windows. The first window shows my past in a different light. The middle window shows the unknown present. The third shows a powerful future. * The potential of each of these times shines through even within this prison. I look through each one for a glimmer of these realities. The act of looking starts to shift the old pain patterns. * I slowly descend, noticing that many of the rooms have grown quiet. The anguish is no longer tangible. When I do sense some activity, I send forgiveness to those that caused the original wounding. * I leave the tower, I look back and breathe deeply. I feel free and open. * I raise my arm to call down lightning to destroy this tower. Even within the fiery flames, I forgive all those who have hurt me or taught me how to fear rather than love. * The tower finally explodes. I breathe and sense myself without any stories at all. I choose from here."

The Tower Intention

Which intention is needed now to heal experiences or relationships that have blown up recently. This portal can rid the toxicity of patterns that have prevented true growth.

The Tower Ritual Suggestion

Use Calling the Circle as the structure for the ceremony. Bring a few pictures that symbolize times of being loved. Place these in a circle around the center seat. Once seated in the center, read your intention aloud to your Divine Allies and Beloved Ancestors.

Choose the Tower card or a copy of one. Using scissors, cut out any falling people. Think of all the times that you were thrown out of comfort zones only to discover a real version of you. Place the falling figures upright. Next, cut out the part of the card that shows the point of lightning's impact on the tower. Engage with the ways in which the Creative Unknown has swerved you onto different paths. Start to cut the tower into tiny pieces. As you do this, express gratitude for all the ways you figured out how to cope or hide to be safe in the past. Honor and release those choices of survival. This ritual won't end these stories, but it can change their endings.

Finally, choose three cards to represent:

1. your recognition and awareness of the old ways to be safe,

2. an insight to clearing these from your system,

3. and the advice to have a life free of these default choices.

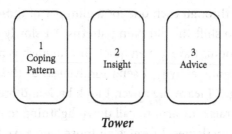

1
Coping
Pattern

2
Insight

3
Advice

Tower

The Star Ritual

The Star Portal

Self-acceptance

Faith

Peace after the storm

The Star Shadow

Cynicism

Judgmental of yourself and others

Refusing to do any introspection

No dreams

The Star Preparation

FINDING THE INTENT—BODY WISDOM

Find fifteen minutes daily to meditate—sitting, walking, or lying.

Centering prayer is a strong, useful tradition. Choose a meaningful term to be your mantra, your sacred word, as a central focus through an entire meditation.

As you meditate, gently shift back to this anchoring word if your mind wanders.

The word could be derived from the Star card itself.

Ask your body what makes it feel like shining.

FINDING THE INTENT—WRITING PROMPTS

Pick five cards and place them in a star formation. Let these cards stimulate thoughts about healing from any tower experience.

What are you finally accepting about yourself or life?

In what ways do you want to shine?

What dream returns in various forms?

FINDING THE INTENT—JOURNEY

"I stand on a path heading toward gentle hills. It is night. The stars start to glimmer. I recognize some familiar constellations. * I notice one star, however, that has many points. It is like no other. It appears to blink at times. * I walk in its direction. I pass through the gentle hills. The silence is rich. * I enter a valley full of flowers. A huge lake glistens under the indigo night sky. There are two water vessels near the pond. * I remove all of my clothes. I balance easily as I kneel with my left knee firmly on the land and my right foot in the refreshing water. * I hold the vessels, and the water starts to move through me as it pours from both. * I am part of a flow that I don't understand, but trust. * The many-pointed star appears to pulse. My spirit and body are one in this holy place."

The Star Intention

What may need to be reset currently? Examine the various aspects of your life. Has there been a major upheaval of any kind? What is needed for a new integration? What new energy has been liberated?

The Star Suggested Ritual

Ideally this ritual would be done under a star-laden night. If that isn't possible, consider doing the ritual after a soak in the tub. Open with Calling the Circle. Sit in the center and envision the crown of your head as a ring of stars. Open fully to the night sky. Speak your intention out loud. After some silence, lay six to eight cards facedown in a star pattern. Allow this to be the star pointing to your destiny. Turn over each card and let it whisper an insight. Do a further reading with all the cards. Look at the way they may all speak to one theme or idea. Find repeating ideas or images. Take on a bird's-eye view of the cards as they speak together.

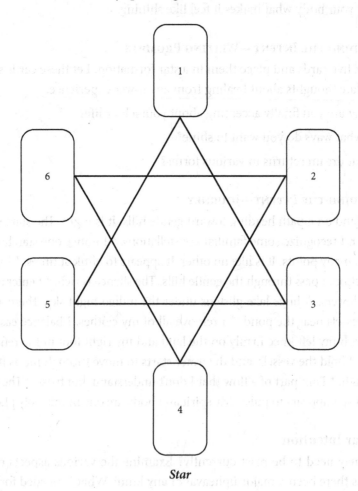

Star

The Moon Ritual

The Moon Portal

Cycles

Illusions

Mystery

The Moon Shadow

Bad timing

Disconnected from your own natural food or sleep rhythms

Can't sense your gut instincts

The Moon Preparation

FINDING THE INTENT—BODY WISDOM

Explore various rhythms through strong dance forms such as ballroom
or tango.

Experiment with your own movements with international music or sing-
ing different rhythms.

Do Yin Yoga to practice going in deeper with one pose.

Ask your body how it shape-shifts.

FINDING THE INTENT—WRITING PROMPTS

Pull one card and write about its deepest mystery for you. Invent a sto-
ryline if there isn't an obvious one present.

Describe a prophecy that highly impacted your life.

How do you need to get wild?

How does your feminine nature of reception balance with the masculine
nature of manifestation?

FINDING THE INTENT—JOURNEY

"I stand on a path that meanders between two gray towers. * The moon is
in her full glory. There is illumination a few feet all around me but anything
in the distance is not clear. * As I walk, I hear someone calling my name in
a muffled tone. I would be frightened if it wasn't so lovely and strong. * My

stress starts to melt away. I feel beautiful and strong with each step. My legs want to run. * I sense animals nearby. We are all loved by this moon. * As I pass between the two towers, it feels like another dimension of time and space. * The path goes to the edge of an ocean. My whole being moves as one with the rhythm of the waves. I lose sense of myself altogether. I am free of all stories. * I become large. I allow my mythic self to emerge freely."

The Moon Intention

Imagine being in full alignment with the moon. What could evolve with time, focus, and energy? Use this intention for great magic and mystery.

The Moon Suggested Ritual

Consider a ritual that would be concurrent with a complete moon cycle. Within this timeline of twenty-eight days, the intention could be presented in a few ways.

You could repeat the full intention four times during four phases of the moon—dark (unknown), new (beginning), full (prime), and waning (tying up loose ends). Sense the difference with each repetition. Let your understanding deepen as you bring the intention under each phase of the moon.

Another variation is to structure an intention into four phases. Each phase would have a specific part of the intention. The dark moon is a meditative time to receive insights. The new moon is a time for stating your desired wish. Ask for any actions/shifts that are needed leading up to the full moon. On the full moon, open to blessings and activation of the intention. During the waning moon, let go of all attachments with gratitude. Be with what is.

On the new moon, observe Calling the Circle. Once in center, draw three cards or use your own moon spread. Display the cards chosen until the next dark moon. Track all messages received. Create a plan or revise the intention if needed.

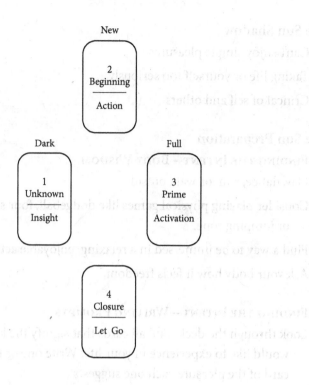

New

2
Beginning

Action

Dark

1
Unknown

Insight

Full

3
Prime

Activation

4
Closure

Let Go

New Moon Messages

1

2

3

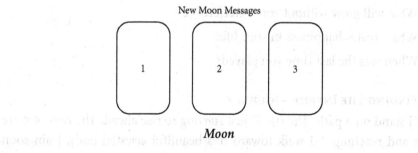

Moon

The Sun Ritual

The Sun Portal
Joy

Simplicity

Mindfulness

Growth

The Sun Shadow

Can't enjoy simple pleasures

Taking life or yourself too seriously

Critical of self and others

The Sun Preparation

FINDING THE INTENT—BODY WISDOM

Play, dance, run, or walk outside.

Consider playing physical games like dodgeball, four square,
    or jumping rope.

Find a way to be immersed in a relaxing, enjoyable activity.

Ask your body how it feels freedom.

FINDING THE INTENT—WRITING PROMPTS

Look through the deck. Pull all cards that signify the kind of joy you
    would like to experience in your life. Write one or two paragraphs per
    card of the pleasure each one suggests.

What will grow without your interference?

What creates happiness in your life?

When was the last time you played?

FINDING THE INTENT—JOURNEY

"I stand on a path. The sun is just starting to rise ahead. The rays of it are
long and reaching. * I walk toward this beautiful celestial body. I am soon
joined by a beautiful white horse. I sense this creature inviting me to ride. *
We enter an area of green and sunflowers surrounded by an ancient gray wall.
* I feel increased warmth and aliveness as the sun slowly rises. My body is
happy. * I raise my arms and bring in rays of light. * There is laughter nearby
and the sounds of content people. * I am safe. I am alive."

The Sun Intention

Pay heed to triggers or recollections of being lonely, disconnected, or depressed
that may have surfaced during the preparation phase. Sun magic can certainly

heal old wounds and pains. Often, the Sun card imagery features a child. The intention could come from this place of your own innocence.

The Sun Ritual Suggestion

Before opening a Calling the Circle ritual, look through the tarot deck for desired qualities, energies, and gifts that reflect the intention. Now go through the deck once more for the cards that reflect ways that may prevent the intention's potential. On a huge piece of paper, draw a circle. Within it, write the full intention and a few words of each of the desirable cards. On the outside of the circle, write the undesired triggers and descriptions. Open the four quarters in Calling the Circle. As you take your place in the center, read the intention and the desired qualities out loud. Make a symbolic sacrifice of the undesired ones by cutting each one away until only the circle remains. Be creative with that which you do not want—bury, rip up, or burn them. Post the circle until the next significant solar event, such as an equinox or solstice.

Judgement Ritual

Judgement Portal

Healing

Marching orders

Renewal

Karma

Judgement Shadow

Deny your true calling

Feel no sense of purpose

Feel frozen or stuck

Judgement Preparation

FINDING THE INTENT—BODY WISDOM

Use a meditative process such as guided meditation of your chakras or an anatomy coloring book.

Learn more about your body. An acupuncturist, healer, herbalist, or
some other alternative modality professional might be able to offer
new insights.

Ask your body how it wants you to trust its healing process.

FINDING THE INTENT—WRITING PROMPTS

Think of what the trajectory of your life might be from this point until
the day you die. Pull three cards about the possibilities that are yours
to use this time well.

Do you have a strong sense of feeling new? If not, when was the last time
you did?

Describe the initiation or rite of passage that you might be currently
experiencing.

How is the Creative Unknown calling you?

What or who would you serve without hesitation?

What has returned in a new form?

FINDING THE INTENT—JOURNEY

"I am standing on a path. It feels slightly strange. The sun brings needed
warmth as I start to walk. * I take in the surroundings that feel strangely like
some other planet. * There is a sound of some beautiful melody in the distance. It starts to grow. I'm not sure if it is a part of nature itself or if music is
being played. * As I walk, I feel light, long, and loose all over. My feet seem
to barely touch the ground. * I am certain that the sound is coming through
the clouds up ahead. I start to float. * I rise up to the clouds. Other forms are
doing the same. * I see powerful visions of my destiny. I enter this dream.
* I remember that I am spirit. Our forms seem to dissolve into particles of
light. I return to love. * I lose all sense of time. * As if waking from a dream, I
find myself eventually coming back into my body. I descend easily and touch
ground. * I hear the melody within my heart now as I walk back to the point
where I appeared."

Judgement Intention

Vision is needed before any effective strategy can be put into place. Go deep within to create a vision of a loved life. Use Judgement as a portal to direct your energy and time.

Judgement Ritual Suggestion

Judgement presents a particular portal of a significant rite of passage. Within Calling the Circle, name the four quarters as four aspects of this intention. For example: east is the beginning awareness, south is the progression or challenge of the intention, west is the necessary transformation, and north is the full manifestation. The center is the integration of all these aspects. Choose a tarot card for each of these stations. Allow time to listen to the calling. What is being asked of you?

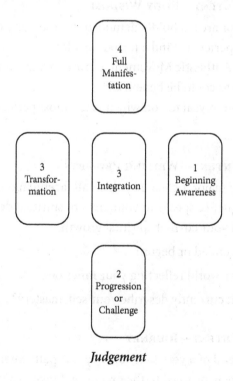

Judgement

The World Ritual

The World Portal

Integration

Completion

Service

The World Shadow

Imposter syndrome

Avoiding stillness

Can't sense achievement for a job well done

The World Preparation

FINDING THE INTENT—BODY WISDOM

The World major arcana boldly demonstrates the unity of a spirit having a human experience. Find a form that allows your body to lead freely and deeply. Authentic Movement, chair dancing, contact improvisation, and butō could be beneficial.

Ask your body to reveal to you why it is the most perfect form of your spirit.

FINDING THE INTENT—WRITING PROMPTS

Shuffle only the major arcana. Lay them all faceup in one long line. This random sequence speaks to your current spiritual development.
Write about your current spiritual growth.

What cycle has ended or begun?

How is the outer world reflecting your inner one?

How would you currently describe your self-mastery?

FINDING THE INTENT—JOURNEY

"I stand at the end of a very long journey. * A path emerges leading to the edge of a cliff. I slowly proceed to the precipice. I take in a panoramic view of a rugged landscape below. * I recall all of the people and places I have loved. * My heart beats loudly with each memory and breath. * As my gratitude grows, I see an image of myself as pure spirit in the sky before me. * I have a clear sense of this current point in my life. I know how I got here. I know where I would like to go next. * The spirit comes to a still point, yet there is movement. I feel myself vibrate as pure energy. * I am one with myself, my life, and source."

The World Intention
Any self-limiting beliefs create a state of separateness. Create an intention that transforms any conditioned beliefs into an affirming sense of self. Being truly spirit-led is one of self-compassion, wholeness, and curiosity.

The World Ritual Suggestion
Choose five to seven cards that depict a fulfillment of your intention. Open Calling the Circle. The four quarters symbolize the elemental world: air—angel, fire—lion, water—eagle, and earth—ox. Stand in the center as spirit—the dancer. Read your intention out loud three times. Hold one of the chosen tarot cards. See a bright light from the card itself. Imagine the light going through all four corners of Earth and attracting the people and experiences that are needed. The journey of the light ends in your heart. Let it bless you and this intention. Repeat with all of the chosen cards. Allow the color of the light to change with each one. You are the center, the co-creator, and the recipient. Take your time. Involve some physicality if possible. After the ritual, take note of strong, visceral insights.

Summary
In this chapter, we explored each major arcana as a portal of wisdom, power, and magic. The 22 Acts of Magic template contains numerous prompts, questions, descriptions, and ideas to gain the magic needed through a well-crafted intention. The suggestions for both the ritual and the usage of tarot are only that: suggestions. May they inspire a ritual created and directed by your own guidance.

Chapter Five
DEEPENING RITUALS FOR ONE

The major arcana rituals of the previous chapter are symbolic steps through powerful portals. Within this chapter, rituals and ideas are presented to develop self-awareness and growth, the portal of self. Working with divinatory tools such as tarot requires one to be centered within one's body, mind, and spirit. There are also rituals honoring other lifetimes, Beloved Ancestors, dreams, Divine Allies, and your Destiny Self. Let us start with the magician's table of tools—the altar.

An altar creates a visual center of tangible mystery. This designated area holds space for the Creative Unknown as a foundation piece for rituals. A seasonal theme for the altar that includes symbolic objects such as photos of loved ones, rocks, soil from beloved lands, and your tarot card of the day (COTD, pg 34), creates a daily focus and gratitude. The first decision is of finding the right location. Any place where you routinely spend time is fruitful. I have a small kitchen altar. It is in direct visual line as I wash dishes. People tend to build altars in their bedrooms since it tends to be the most private room. Bedrooms can be tricky, however. If you lose sleep or start having very odd dreams, find another place. A portable altar is great because it can be placed anywhere to be accessible for ritual use. Consider creating one with a shoebox or some kind of stand.

Another gesture for mystery to become more conscious is calling for a guide. Whether they are a loved one who has passed, a Divine Ally, an angelic being, an animal totem, Blessed Ancestor, or all of the above, our spirit always works in conjunction with someone or something else. Unlike our human nature, which tends to live in separation, our spirit exists in unity with the source of love. Using the Power of Pretend will help greatly since it is a leap of faith to trust that which we cannot see and touch. The Guide ritual will assist in this process.

Guide Ritual

The structure of this ritual is based on Calling the Circle (pg 17). Approach the ritual as an initiate. You might consider wearing something symbolic such as white or an accessory of your ancestors. What would one wear to meet a new friend? After you have opened the directions and settled in the center, ask for a Divine Ally to join you. Be open to whomever would come to help you navigate a life of being spirit-led. Once you feel an energy of trust and safety, ask for their name and image. Don't question or second-guess the response.

When reading for clients, I often sense a group of guides. The group seems to change with the seeker's various learning curves. This divine committee of sorts is a larger way of seeing the way your spirit is supported and connected. Rather than calling one guide, ask for all loving influences currently in your life. As you stand in the center, relax with slow, silent, and soft breaths for five to ten minutes. Imagine yourself in a large space. Ask for those who are at your side from other realms. Open your mind and heart as you receive a number of guides. Who would you want to enter? Imagining may feel false but opening sacred space and allowing forms of love to protect and bless you is a direct route. This committee will serve you well if you can access them regularly through meditation or by request in times of need. Grounding (pg 12) and calling the guides to mind before divination or during ritual is a winning combination. Spend time with one or all of them at the beginning of the day for guidance, or at the end of the day in gratitude. Spiritual support is more easily envisioned with the visual aid of an altar and the partnership of divine guides.

Your well-being is of major importance. In the plethora of offerings of self-growth and development, the weeklong exploration called the Hoffman Process is a potent learning of the self. This technique focuses on the release of shame absorbed as a child and is a process that values a spirit-led life. One underlying principle of the Hoffman Process is that we are comprised of four parts: the spirit, intellect, emotional self, and the body. Their term for this is "Quadrinity." The following ritual is a variation of the Hoffman Process to honor these four spheres every morning.

Quadrinity Ritual

The body, intellect, emotional self, and spirit dance together. The dance is harmonious when spirit leads. Shortly after you wake up, sit quietly with your cards. Become aware of your body. Scan for any sensations such as tightness or tingling. Observe without judgment all of the ways your body works for you. What does your body appear to be experiencing? Ask if there is anything your body wants or needs from you today. After receiving a feeling, thought, image, color, or whatever comes in response, pull one card and lay it facedown. Thank your body out loud.

Gently shift your awareness to your intellect. This self will most likely look just like you but is composed of pure thought, memory, and communication. What scene has been playing out in your mind? Ask your intellect what it needs or wants from you today. Pull one card once you sense the request. Don't be surprised with odd responses. You aren't in charge, you are simply the cosmic journalist of sorts. Thank your intellect out loud for being your navigator in the world.

Gently shift your awareness to your emotional self. This aspect of your emotions and vision could also look like you but possibly at a different age. If your heart was an actor onstage, what scene is being revealed? What has your body been going through lately? Ask what this self wants or needs from you today. Choose the card facedown that feels close to the energy of their response. Thank your emotional self for processing life.

Breathe. Let each breath become a beautiful light that fills your entire being. This light is your spirit. Once you sense you are immersed in this light, what message does your spirit have for you today? Choose a card facedown. Thank your spirit.

Sense your guide's hand on your shoulder. Allow yourself to feel their support fully. Ask for a message you could use for today. Pull a card. Thank them.

Now take a few minutes to turn over the cards, keeping them in order. Let each one affirm or enhance the various aspects' responses. Some may offer different messages. This ritual alone could be a bedrock spiritual practice if you integrate the messages given during the day.

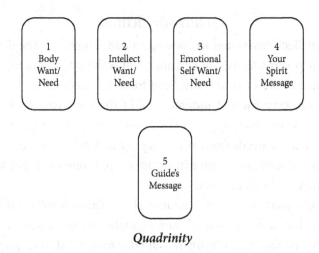

Quadrinity

There are other ways to check in as spirit and human. The body is the form of spirit. It is the five-pointed star, the pentagram. The body with spirit is a dance of matter and energy. Through the centuries, a structure of the body and spirit is that of the chakras. Originating in ancient Indian philosophy, each chakra is an energy center deep within the core of the body, along the spine, and through the crown of the head. Consider chakras as crossroads where mental, emotional, and energetic aspects meet. Each of the seven chakras not only have their own sound and location but color and symbol as well.

First Chakra
Red

Base of spine

Earth, ancestor support, support, work, resources, foundation

Second Chakra
Orange

Sacral

Sexuality, creativity, expression

Third Chakra
Yellow

Just below the navel

Will, direction, power

Fourth Chakra
Green

Heart and center of the chest

Everyone and everything, source, giving and receiving love

Fifth Chakra
Sky blue

Throat

Truth, communication, devotion, voice

Sixth Chakra
Indigo

Third eye

Wisdom, insight, imagination, vision

Seventh Chakra
Violet
Crown of head

Consciousness, Creative Unknown connection

The following Chakra ritual is particularly effective after a session of stretching, bathing, or a walk.

Chakra Ritual

The chakras themselves are portals. One of each of their aspects—color, sound, or theme—will be an entry point to each chakra in this ritual. To start, set aside fifteen or thirty minutes, and get comfortable in a sitting or lying position with the cards nearby. Focus on the chakras one by one, imagining each as a small sphere of its color and location. Consider its theme as you breathe into that space. During the meditation, allow messages and images to surface.

Pull one card for a chakra as you finish envisioning it. Interpret the cards after the entire meditation. The cards chosen will reflect an insight into the current state of that particular energy center and your being as a whole.

Lay the chosen cards in the order of the chakras in one long line. Look at the overall pattern first. Notice any suit, family, or number that is completely absent. What is missing is as important as what has surfaced, which will indicate a need for an overall balance. Then take note of your immediate sensations with each card. If one seems particularly concerning, is it reflecting that area in your life? For example, if you chose the Tower card for the throat chakra, this may indicate the need to speak about something that has been troubling you. The major arcana may show huge amounts of energy while the court cards may speak to someone who is a strong influence on that sphere.

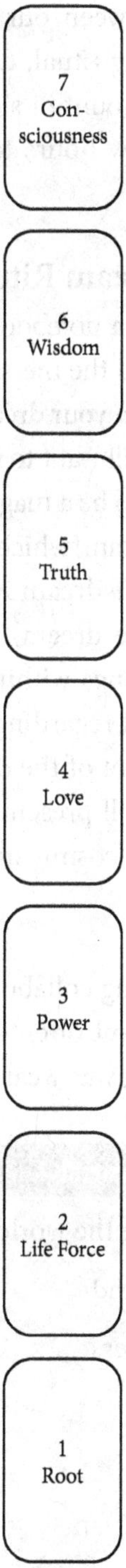

7
Con-
sciousness

6
Wisdom

5
Truth

4
Love

3
Power

2
Life Force

1
Root

Chakra

Another organic connection between our spirit and human selves is that of the dream world. The following ritual, designed to help you develop that connection, will require a fair amount of sleep. A deficit in sleep starves the mind's regeneration, so add a few hours to your sleep regimen if possible before doing this ritual.

Dream Ritual

Write your question or request in a notebook and place it near your bed. Pull one card. Do not try to understand the message. Trust that this card will be an entry into what will be illustrated in your dream. Be prepared to write or record the dream while half asleep; you will want to record it as soon as you wake. This may happen at 3 a.m. That seems to be a magical time for waking. Make sure to include how you felt during the dream, which is key to the insight needed.

At a later time, deconstruct the dream into columns. In the first column, create a sequential outline of the dream, using the individual events that occurred and people or other beings within it. In the second column, write the first thing that comes to mind regarding each item in column one. Draw a random card for each component of the dream, and record this in column three. These layers of meaning will present the message of the dream using your unconscious, conscious, and cosmic input.

Example

I want to know about an upcoming collaborative project. I received the Two of Swords before sleeping. I dreamt of entering a movie theater. The movie audience was blue dogs. Each dog was wearing a fez. I felt mildly surprised.

Dream Item	My Initial Thought	Card Chosen
Go to movies	Escape the world	Seven of Wands
Movie theater	My mind	Six of Cups
Audience	Watchers	Three of Wands
Dogs	Circus	Page of Pentacles
Blue	Sky	The Emperor
Fez	Steely Dan	The Hermit

First, the Two of Swords spoke to my feeling that the project is at a stand-still. I felt as if I am waiting for marching orders. For the cards drawn for each dream item:

1. Go to movies; escape the world; Seven of Wands: There are a lot of creative ideas flying around but it doesn't feel real yet. Are we just pretending?
2. Movie theater; my mind; Six of Cups: I need to go to a sweet space within so I can create and easily share my ideas.
3. Audience; watchers; Three of Wands: This project will have a magic of its own and will appeal to many.
4. Dogs; circus; Page of Pentacles: Our audience is willing to take a risk. They are young, loyal, and enjoy the absurd.
5. Blue; sky; the Emperor: Do not underestimate their intelligence. Be as creative as possible.
6. Fez; Steely Dan; the Hermit: This project stands alone in terms of its style. It has a great vibe and depth as well.

This exercise helped me value my own contributions to the project. The messages about it being a fresh idea created a new sense of confidence. I was able to release a feeling of being stuck.

Dreams in combination with the cards can make powerful connections that might have been dismissed as vivid imagination. If you can name it, you can claim it!

Light/Shadow/Dark Ritual

A ritual that can help discover hidden knowledge is by making use of your light, dark, and shadow selves. This particular ritual is effective during solstices and equinoxes. Whether done as an exercise or engaged within a sacred space using the Calling the Circle ritual, this process uncovers information from the unconscious.

Take some time to ground. Mindfully separate the entire deck into these three groups: the Light Self, the Shadow Self, and the Dark Self. Define these three classifications yourself or use the following:

- The Light Self—All aspects of love, trust, safety, and joy
- The Shadow Self—The unknown, or hidden skills, gifts, and beliefs
- The Dark Self—Egoist needs, desires, and power

There are three ways to process these groups for a better understanding of yourself. First, look through each group and list words or phrases that seem to stand out. There will likely be repetition in themes. Second, randomly select one card from each group. Detect any overall pattern of your current energy by looking at all three together. The third method is consciously choosing one card from the Light Self group of something that you truly desire to experience. Choose the one card from the Shadow Self group that is most confusing or bewildering. Choose from the Dark Self group a card that scares or frightens you. How do these three cards relate to each other? Allow all three to speak clearly to you about what is needed in your life.

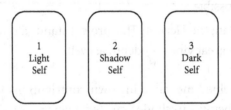

Light/Shadow/Dark

Hopefully, tarot is becoming a strong GPS of sorts for directing energies and focus in loving your life. As you may have experienced in the Light/ Shadow/Dark ritual, hidden patterns and insights are surfaced. With awareness, effective integration can take place.

Vision Ritual

A spirit-led life needs a mindful focus and effective self-awareness. The Vision ritual provides the creation of this commitment to reveal your real potential such as those uncovered by the Light/Shadow/Dark ritual.

Choose cards from your deck that represent what your life might be like if certain self-limiting situations or patterns ended. What would life feel like without current chronic patterns, unfulfilling relationships of yourself and others, or an unsettling state of being? Narrow this selection to those essential needs and wants that are required to live a life with no regrets. You could use the information you gathered from the Light/Shadow/Dark ritual. Over the next few days, write about the ideal day of this imagined life.

Start with the moment you wake up until you go to sleep. Use the images, ideas, and essences from your chosen cards. Keep the scenarios deliberately general without any names.

For example, I chose the Three of Wands, the Two of Cups, and the World. My ideal day of that future life would entail waking up in a loved one's arms. That day, I need to do work that is satisfying and purposeful. I start to gather things together for a trip to work with strong colleagues the following weekend. We are creating a system to help divination become more accessible. If you can "see" it, you can be it.

After the vision, create a few action steps or a commitment to making this life a reality. This vision statement can be utilized well by speaking it aloud every morning as a powerful affirmation. It can also be used in the following ritual that explores your soul in various dynamics—the House of Soul ritual.

If we are indeed a spirit having a human experience, what if the human self is actually composed of a thousand selves? Imagine the various roles you play in a lifetime: sibling, partner, worker, lover, etc. Multiply those roles, or "selves" across lifetimes. Envision each of these experiences as so necessary and complete that they appear as three-dimensional beings. For example, any chronic problem may indicate a personal trauma from this life or some other life. Using the Power of Pretend, allow that issue to be an actual psyche self whom you could have a dialogue with for a better understanding of the origin of the discomfort. As a group, these selves all reside in your soul. With each life, all experiences are recorded. Accessing this in a more visual way is seeing all of these personalities as they reside in your own House of Soul.

The House of Soul contains all of your soul's experiences and lessons of every incarnation, both past and future as well as the present. It is an imagined personal wing of the Akashic records library, a metaphysical concept of a repository of each soul's journey through all of time. You are the only one who can enter this "house."

House of Soul Ritual

Before the ritual, do the Grounding ritual (pg 12). Craft a two- to three-sentence vision or simply use the one from the Vision ritual. You will be entering the House of Soul as your current incarnation to form a strong alliance with those parts of you that will hopefully help your vision become a true reality. This is a sacred cast of an inner theater. Give the selves broad titles such as the lover, the scared one, or the doubting one. You are the lead character only in that you have a body and consciousness. Your main objective is to clearly state your heart vision and ask what the selves need or want to help you accomplish it.

First, consider familiar obstacles. One way to surface these aspects is to take note of any doubts when you read the vision aloud. A common doubt concerns the resources needed for our dreams. In this case, you may want to invite the accountant, the poor one, the cynical one, etc., to speak with you at the negotiating table. Another consideration is to invite a self or selves that may have a positive influence in making this vision a reality. If you want to succeed in a particular art, you may want to ask the star, the past life artist, the networker, the magical one, etc.

When you have your vision in hand and determine which selves could be strong allies in making it happen, fan out your cards facedown in front of you.

Read the following journey, pausing briefly for every *. Alternatively, you could make an audio recording of the text and pauses to play back so you can close your eyes the entire time.

"As I close my eyes, I slowly start to breathe slower and lower. It is pleasant as I begin to feel calm. * I envision myself standing and connected to earth. * A mist starts to rise. It is enveloping me in its warmth and fullness. * The mist transports me back to one of my very first incarnations on this planet. * I experience weightlessness. After some time, I sense descending to solid ground. * I remember an amazing first connection to the earth. The mist starts to descend down around my feet. * A structure starts to appear in front of me. It is a house. It initially changes into various structures such as a cabin, a temple, and a mansion. I breathe and wait. It eventually settles into my very own House of Soul. * It was created when my soul was created. I go to the entrance. * Before entering, I place my hands on my heart and speak my heart vision out loud. * I enter the house. All the selves are aware of my entrance. They are excited and curious. * I am drawn to a room that has a beautiful sitting area with at least one round table and two chairs. * I enter the room and sit in one of the chairs. * At this time, I invite a self that may be directly involved in the sphere that needs change. I invite the _____ to join me. * I breathe and patiently wait. I release all preconceptions of who they are or what they will look like. * They enter and take a seat. I welcome them. * I hold my hand over my heart and say my heart vision out loud. I tell them that this is important to me. I will need them to come with me for this vision to come true. I will leave no part of my self behind. * I ask, "What do you want or need from me to fully be with me in creating this heart vision?" * After some time has passed, I receive an image, message, or vision. * Choose one card from the ones fanned out in front of me to affirm or enhance their request. * If it feels correct, we can go further into a dialogue or thank them warmly and offer them a gift. * I call the next self of interest. * When I am finished, I leave a bowl of beautiful objects [crystals, apples, etc.] on the table to signal to all the others within this house that I may speak to them at another time. * I leave the House of Soul to return to the spot where I arrived. * The mist rises up around me to transport me to my current time."

As with any ritual, stay aware for the appearance of dreams, shifts, or synchronicities in the following days. Always leave room for the Creative Unknown to respond fully. With this ritual of many selves and the others, tarot and ritual serve as powerful change agents in perspectives and behaviors. The story or stories we believe in transform us.

Ending the Story Spread

Often, we wish to change the ending of a story, especially those of great sorrow or abrupt endings. Holding grudges, blame, or avoidance continues toxic stories. If you have a couple of bad chapters in your past, the Ending the Story spread may be helpful.

Think of any events or relationships that have ended in the world but not in your heart. These may be relationships that you left, a toxic group dynamic that still stings, or an uncomfortable living situation that still haunts you from time to time. You left, but energetically, the story has not ended. The hurt, anger, or confusion has not been resolved. Which event or relationship popped to mind first?

The spread will have eight cards total. Carefully choose the first three cards that hold the energy of that story before things went bad; each a representation of a time when you were fully engaged and possibly happy. Choose a fourth card to signify that moment of the first red flag, sense of unease, or when you knew it was time to leave.

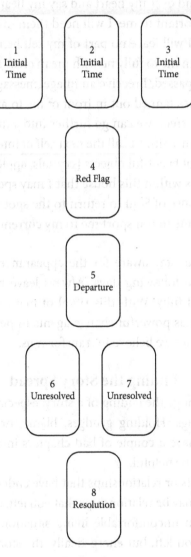

Ending Story

Now choose three cards randomly about your state of being and circumstances regarding the departure. The fifth position gives a message about the departure itself. The sixth and seventh cards speak to that which has been left unresolved. These three will give you a sense of how the story has continued energetically.

Recall this entire episode through the lens of all of these cards. What surprised you most about looking at this memory from the images? What is being triggered? Allow all feelings and sensations to surface with compassion. The observer within needs to support the feeler through this story for it to fully transform. This spread goes beyond just gathering new information. It is surfacing what still needs to be healed.

Pull the eighth and last card for the needed resolution from you to finally close (not slam) this door. Keep in mind that everyone is at fault and no one is to blame. Deeply forgive all actors involved, including yourself. Releasing painful stories makes room for great ones.

Beloved Ancestor Ritual

Stories that feed your well-being can be those of your true origins, the ancestors. Beloved Ancestors make up your four original bloodlines with you as their living representative. Beloved Ancestors are also those of land, art, activism, or other cherished lineage. These are your elders. During these shifting times for ourselves and for others, we need to reconnect more than ever to our beginnings. For the entire ritual, emphasize the title "Beloved" ancestor as an energetic boundary from those ancestors who are not well or are lost.

Use Calling the Circle (pg 17) for the basic structure. Each of the four quarters will represent your four bloodlines: your mother's mothers, mother's fathers, father's fathers, and father's mothers. Adding photos, a map, or food or drink from their origins will help you visualize. If honoring the Beloved Ancestors not of your blood, designate the quarters in a way that feels right for you. Place one candle in each quarter.

At each station, formally introduce yourself by saying your full name and your position in the family: "I am the child of [*full names of your parents or chosen surrogate.*]" Light the candle with honor and humility.

Take your place in the center. Envision a Plexiglas box completely surrounding you. It will act as protection from those ancestors who may hear your call but are not in beloved status since they haven't found their way back to their beloved tribe. Breathe deeply as you open your heart to each direction. Pull one card for each direction. These cards will act as direct messages from that set of ancestors.

After receiving four messages, take a seat in the center. Focus on your first chakra at the base of your spine. Release any fear, concern, and unwanted beliefs. Take some time to be thoroughly open to the four messages. Remain open and curious. Ask for the support and blessings of the Beloved Ancestors to be their true representative. When it feels finished, thank each group as you move counterclockwise blowing out the candles. The four cards chosen may reveal more information at a later time. Again, stay aware of shifts, changes, and dreams in the upcoming weeks.

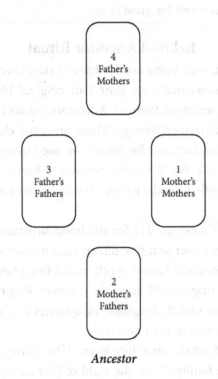

4
Father's
Mothers

3
Father's
Fathers

1
Mother's
Mothers

2
Mother's
Fathers

Ancestor

Destiny Self Ritual

We have talked about your self, your many selves, and your ancestral self. One more self that can truly offer helpful guidance is your Destiny Self. This future self has manifested this life's destiny starting from this moment. This is not who you will become by default but rather by fearless love.

Select a special time to do this ritual, such as your birthday or a relevant astrological alignment. Have all the major arcana faceup in a big circle encompassing the center seat. Have the minor cards in one pile within reach. Use the Calling the Circle ritual (pg 17) as the basic structure; create sacred space by opening the quarters. Make your way to sit in the center facing the World card.

Set a timer for fifteen minutes. Go within as you envision traveling to your future self. Imagine and ask to meet your Destiny Self the day before they die. Use the Power of Pretend to imagine who you would be at this last point of your life if you lived fearlessly in love from your current age. Release any of your own fears or misconceptions about your appearance or power.

Once you can imagine this meeting, you are encouraged to have an easy dialogue. If you have no questions of your own, consider asking them what you are currently doing that is totally on the pulse, off track, or not on the radar at all in terms of becoming them. Pull one card for each of these focuses to help affirm their message at a later time. Return from the meditation once the allotted time is over. Close the circle with gratitude. The chosen cards affirm the messages received or deliver brand new insights.

The very first time I met my future self, I was fifty years old. She called me a spring chicken. Compared to her, I am indeed young. It forever changed my concept of being old. With this new insight, I realized how I had started thinking "old." I decided to exercise more, change up my clothes, and wear pretty shoes.

Summary

This chapter offered rituals that dig deep beyond your rational and conscious awareness. Symbolic gestures such as building your own altar, asking for a specific guide or committee of guides, and the spiritual practice of the Quadrinity ritual fortify a daily focus on being spirit-led. Systems such as the chakras, dream interpretation, and shadow work surface unconscious needs. The Vision ritual is a statement for creating a life you desire. You negotiate your true vision with various aspects of yourself for better awareness and integration in the House of Soul ritual.

A great deal of energy can be transformed with the Ending the Story spread and connecting with our roots in the Beloved Ancestor ritual. The final ritual is meeting and gathering advice from your future self who truly fulfills destiny.

Chapter Six
RITUALS FOR READING FOR OTHERS

We are both the storyteller and the story. The rituals of the last chapter surfaced stories that need to be created, released, or changed. In this chapter, the rituals are designed to surface others' stories. Initially, we will look at the necessity of keeping vital boundaries and knowing one's biases through the Bias-Free spread and the Zip It ritual. The rest of the chapter are spreads and rituals under the umbrella of the six principles, a powerful backbone for any kind of divination work when reading for another.

Divination is its own form of communication and there are three significant differences from our daily dialogue. First, normally when we speak to one another, we expect the conversation to make sense. It is unlikely that you would engage in an incoherent conversation for long. Second, there are times when we expect the other to back up or explain their position. This need for clarity is particularly helpful if there is confusion or need for more information. If a friend called and simply stated that they are quite upset, you would naturally ask questions. Third, both people in the conversation need to know why they are participating. Is there an expectation of an action, an invitation, or just chitchat?

Divine communication is the opposite of these conversational expectations. First, divine conversation certainly does not always make sense. It may make perfect sense six months from now but not always in the present moment. Second, the reader cannot back up the source of the information if intuitive information flows with the card interpretations.

The last difference from traditional conversation can be the most challenging for the reader. We may be able to detect patterns of the Creative Unknown but interpretation does not assume the understanding of spirit. Both reader and seeker will know what they really want, however the reader cannot be attached to any outcome. For example, if a seeker is nervous about the possibility of losing their job, don't assume this is a bad scenario. We don't know what spirit has up its sleeve. Divine communication as a gathering of messages from deeper patterns is vastly different than doing the other's soul work. The reader needs to approach any answer without attachment to framing the messages as good or bad. Holding the space of neutrality is paramount. Grounding is essential to create this ability.

Bias-Free Spread

Keeping an awareness of one's own biases is a worthy skill to hone. Labeling cards as positive or negative surfaces your own biases. As do people, all cards have both strengths and weaknesses. Barbara Moore, a prolific tarot author and creator, designed the Bias-Free spread to defy projection.

Use the Path spread (pg 37) as the basic structure. The Bias-Free spread is a potent spread when considering various options, such as where to move. To begin, write each of the viable choices on separate slips of paper. Give thought to adding a slip representing an unknown mystery. Fold the papers so the text is hidden. Shuffle the slips well. Place them folded in a vertical line.

Have the seeker shuffle the cards as they focus on their options. Have them lay a card facedown above each of the slips of paper. Each card will give a message of the likely outcome for that particular choice. Gather a clear sense of the results by reading the cards first. After all the cards have been examined, open each slip to reveal the specific situation. Not only does the ritual bypass bias, it also shows a number of paths clearly.

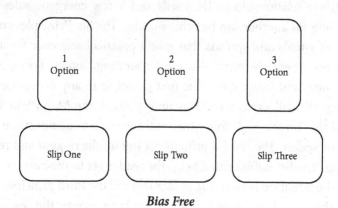

Bias Free

Zip It Ritual

Effective boundaries are needed to create safety and neutrality, sidestep biases, and remain energetically vital. Whether you are reading for someone face-to-face or via phone or internet, it is always an interchange of energy. The format may vary but the boundaries need to be in place for energy to remain vital and insightful. A concept that may help you not try to fix or improve others is to consider that indeed everyone is healing at their best in this moment. Strong boundaries enhance one's ability to be kind, curious, and truthful.

Energetic boundaries extend to one's body as well. One of the most valuable pieces of wisdom I ever received as a reader is the following chakra technique.

The first three chakras (pg 99) are personal and private. As the fourth chakra, the heart is the connection to all others and it can give and receive all love safely. Before reading for another, imagine a giant invisible zipper that runs from your pelvic floor all the way up the center of your body to your crown. See in your mind's eye zipping up your first three chakras (the root, sacral, and solar plexus chakras), all the way up to your heart chakra. The heart, the center of unity and connection for all of us, is designed for vital reciprocity. You may wish to take this a step further and visualize a green ray between you and the seeker's heart centers.

Six Principles

With a strong relationship to the cards and a few energetic safeguards in place, reading for another can be otherworldly. The Six Principles consists of a number of rituals and spreads that give a practical sequence for any form of divination. These six principles are Grounding, Intent, Form, Synchronicity, Closure, and Integration. The first principle in any divination work is Grounding. We will explore the Welcoming ritual, the Moon/Sun Welcome ritual, and the Throne Welcome ritual as three ways to demonstrate grounding with the seeker. The second principle is Intent, the request and reason for the reading. The Fat Rabbit ritual helps the reader get to the heart of the matter. Once the intention is clear, the reader will use the third principle of Form, choosing the spreads or ways to lay the cards to receive the response. The Five Card spread and the Current Cycle spread both work nicely to start any reading as an overview snapshot of the seeker's current energies. During the reading, the Mirror ritual has the seeker interact as a reader. The fourth principle, Synchronicity, is the Creative Unknown's response for any divination. This is the heart of the reading, channeling the responses from the Creative Unknown through the cards. When the reading is nearly done, the fifth principle of Closure is required as a transition from sacred space to world time. The Moon/Sun Closure ritual and Throne Closure ritual are fitting bookends. The sixth principle of Integration encourages the seeker in ways to make use of the insights received.

Before beginning any grounding exercise, take some time for an easy dialogue with your seeker. It would help to briefly describe your process and what they can expect during and from the session. I will often mention that the reading is not a monologue. The seeker can ask questions or shift the direction of questioning at any time.

Grounding—The First Principle

Creating sacred space to invite the Creative Unknown can only be achieved if you are fully present. The process of grounding is necessary. Without it, one tends to be in their head or lose focus. Witnessing and listening skills are compromised if you cannot be in stillness.

There are a multitude of grounding exercises with breath, visualization, silence, and counting down from ten to one. The goal is simple: to become present in body, heart, and mind.

Besides becoming present through grounding as a reader, the following ritual will promote stillness for the seeker. The Welcoming ritual is a basic journey to guide the seeker in grounding. This is sufficient alone in creating sacred space for the two of you. There are two additional rituals, however, that deepen the grounding process. The Moon/Sun and the Throne Welcoming rituals extend the Welcoming ritual to an extra level of mystery or to calm an anxious seeker.

Welcoming Ritual

To begin, place your fingertips on the deck that sits between the two of you. Lead the seeker through the following grounding journey. Each * indicates where you should pause briefly.

"Please put your fingertips, as many or as few as you want, on the deck. * Close your eyes. * Our bodies can only be in the present moment, so it is their greatest gift for us. * Take a few minutes to let your senses navigate you to being here in this room. * You are not in the future or in the past. * You are here. * What do you hear? * Are you feeling warm or cold? * How do your clothes feel on your skin? * Can you sense any source of light? * How does the chair feel? * If this feels comfortable, allow yourself to go deeper within, like Alice down the rabbit hole. * Breathe."

The seeker has been invited to be fully present in mind, heart, and body. You could continue the grounding journey with either the Moon/Sun or Throne Welcome rituals to transport the seeker to an imagined sense of the Creative Unknown. These two rituals each can also act as magical bookends for any reading by using their closure journeys (pg 123).

If you proceed with the journey of either the Moon/Sun or the Throne Welcome rituals, simply add onto the Welcome Ritual journey by speaking either one of them. As before, when reading this for the seeker, pause when an * is noted.

Moon/Sun Welcome Ritual

The Moon/Sun Welcome ritual expands the Welcoming Ritual by guiding the seeker to an open space to experience either the sun or moon and stars above them. It provides an opportunity for them to release daily concerns and attachments to be fully present during the reading.

"Imagine yourself in an ideal landscape, whether it is real or perceived. * It could be a mountain, a beach, desert, forest, or valley. * Only you are here. * Above you is either the moon and stars, or the sun ... whichever your body needs more of. * Look up at this celestial body. It sends a beam of light down through the crown of your head. * It travels down through your spine like honey through the rest of your body. * This beautiful light goes beyond your body to fill the space around you. * You become just the light. * Gently open your eyes."

Throne Welcome Ritual

Another expansion of the Welcoming Ritual is the Throne Welcome ritual. It carefully guides the seeker to an inner landscape to be seated on an organic throne. This throne symbolizes nature and its ability to support the seeker no matter what their state of being has been.

"Go deep within yourself. * There are many beautiful inner landscapes but choose one of nature where you would most want to be. * This landscape helps you feel connected to nature whether real or perceived. * Perhaps it is a mountain, a beach, desert, forest, or valley. * See yourself walking around in this landscape. * You are alone and safe. * Eventually you will see an organic throne of sorts to sit on. * Sit. * Know that not only are you connected to nature, you are completely supported by her. * Gently open your eyes."

Intent—The Second Principle

The stage has now been set. The Creative Unknown has been invited. All magic follows from intention. The intention in a reading is expressed through the questions. If you prefer to let the cards reflect whatever is to be known at this time without questions however, you may wish to set your own intention such as receiving effective and loving insights.

What is it that the seeker really wants to know? This part of the process is often rushed. Taking the time now to discover the true questions actually creates a more efficient flow of information. So how do we get to the heart of the matter? The next ritual may do the trick nicely.

THE FAT RABBIT RITUAL

Asking the seeker for their questions is akin to letting loose a dozen rabbits. As a reader, you are the fox. Which rabbits are worth the chase? Is there one that is particularly big and juicy? The seeker's questions may seem scattered, vague, or unconnected. Some opening questions that may narrow the scope of the reading are:

- What would help in this session?
- What was your intention when you booked the reading?
- If you had a magic wand, what would you change instantly?
- Are you mainly curious or just want an overview of life these days?

Listen to their responses with all of your senses. All cues count. Tone, body language, and phrasing give a great deal of nonverbal information about the heart of the matter. What is *not* being said? What else are you hearing? Assume nothing. Help find the essence of their needs by asking open-ended questions. For example, "If you could change anything in your life right now, what would it be? What did you secretly hope would be surfaced during the reading?" When was the last time you felt as if you were riding the wave of life well? Summarize their needs in your own words to check for any further clarification before laying any cards. The hunt of mystery can now begin!

Form—The Third Principle

Form is the actual tarot spreads or manner of using the cards through the reading. Starting a reading with a spread that will offer an overview of the seeker's current cycles is highly recommended. The overview can often surface important topics or shine a light on those questions or needs that weren't mentioned. The Creative Unknown may present a bigger picture that could give valuable insights. The overview spreads aren't a necessity but can provide compelling context for the intention or theme of the entire session.

A simple overview spread is the Five Card spread (pg 38). It serves a bigger picture within a tight time frame of fifteen minutes or less. All major arcana present the current influences and energies in their life. The minor arcana show how these influences play out day to day.

Readings that are a half hour to an hour long would benefit greatly from a more thorough overview spread such as the Current Cycle spread. It shows the seeker's current learning curve regarding their life as a whole. It offers a framework for discovering that which might have previously gone undetected during the process of determining their intention for the session.

CURRENT CYCLE SPREAD

Direct the seeker to shuffle the cards and lay any seven cards facedown from left to right. You can then place them in the pattern.

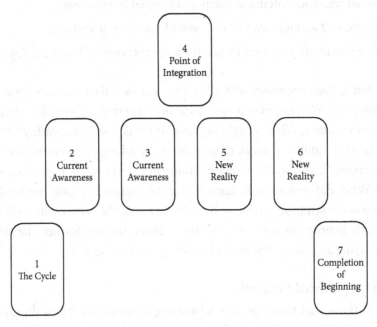

Current Cycle Spread

1. The Cycle: This card speaks to the seeker's current theme. Spirit has deliberately placed them in this cycle for a specific integration.

2 and 3. Current Awareness: Both of these cards present the seeker's current perspectives regarding the theme card. Two cards are helpful because there may be mixed emotions or various states regarding the theme.

4. Point of Integration: Spirit is guiding the seeker to this point of integration. This is the request of the Creative Unknown. What aspect of reality needs to be acknowledged? Notice the differences with insights from cards two and three. How does understanding evolve?

5 and 6. New Reality: As a result of integrating the reality of the fourth card, these two cards present new consequences, shifts, and ideas. The entire integration does not need to be completed to embody new perspectives. New energy sweeps in with awareness. Even more can enter with permission. Notice the difference between the former reality and this new one.

7. Completion/Beginning: This card's position speaks to the ending of this cycle or the heralding of the next one. If it feels entirely different than all the others, it is most likely a glimpse into what is to come.

The core of the reading are spreads that have designated positions or flow organically. Like a good meal, the choice, preparation, presentation, and timing are all dependent on the cook's choices. Take time and stay aware of your own progress toward creating a strong reading from beginning to end. With practice in reading for others, your unique style will be created. All card rituals and spreads throughout this book can be easily adapted to conduct readings for others. For instance, use the Quadrinity ritual (pg 97) for the seeker if they have been experiencing a lot of fear, anxiety, or confusion. It is a helpful ritual to help them feel at home again in their own skin. Fan the cards facedown in front of them. Guide them in visualizing each of their aspects—the body, emotional self, the intellect, and their spirit—asking what each needs or wants from the seeker. Have the seeker receive the response in silence and then randomly chose a card. After all the cards are chosen, have the seeker speak to the direct impressions they received before giving the additional message from each chosen card.

The options available in the Story spreads (pg 36) are dependable vehicles to use through an entire reading. Use as few or as many cards as you want to respond to each topic. Stay open and curious as you follow the narrative being presented. Allow your poetic self to speak. Improvise or create on the spot.

MIRROR RITUAL

Up to this point, you have been the reader interpreting the cards. Let us look at a ritual that involves the seeker as a co-interpreter of the cards.

At times, you can go deeper with the evolving story emerging from the reading if you have the seeker speak to a card's imagery. This is helpful for those topics that are recurring patterns or lifelong fears. Have the seeker shuffle and randomly choose one card as a response to the question, issue, or interest. Instruct them to not show the card or reveal its title. Have them speak about anything they feel, see, or sense from the image. You don't want a literal description of the images but rather how it makes them feel or think. Take notes if needed. When they have finished, ask to see the card. Weave their perception and the tarot message together for a tailor-made response. Their perceptions of the card and your understanding of its meaning together can produce powerful recognitions. For example, the seeker may see in the eight of swords someone that was tied up and abandoned. This might give the reader a strong clue to the challenge this seeker faces in order to believe that they have choices in some aspect of their life.

Synchronicity—The Fourth Principle

This principle is the essence of a reading. It is the divine response from the Creative Unknown. Synchronicity includes the answers, solutions, and prophecies as well as anything that happens during the session. All of your studies, practice, envisioning sacred space, and consecrating the tools lead to this moment. With permission, the needed insights will come from the Creative Unknown, your wisdom, and the patterns of the cards. If your understanding of the source has not been developed, meaningful coincidences will be diminished from not trusting what you can see from all angles. If unsure, use the Power of Pretend to experience full reciprocity with tarot's imagery and divine guidance.

Trust how you perceive each card in the moment. The Entering the Card ritual (pg 25) demonstrated the multitude of ways to perceive one card. During a reading, trust that the layer that is most relevant will call your attention. If you see or sense something, say it. That said, always keep in mind that kindness and compassion will deliver any message correctly.

Trust that everything that happens between opening sacred space and closure are messages as important as any from the cards. Anything that happens between the moment of grounding and the closure is part of the message; an ambulance driving by, a card that flies out, or their cell phone ringing is as much a part of the reading as any card. Interpreting those events is a part of synchronicity.

Keep in mind that simply asking a question does not guarantee an answer. Stay open and engaged. You will be led to the questions and answers that matter most.

Closure—The Fifth Principle

The fifth principle is the one most overlooked even though it is another chance to experience mystery. Near the end of the session, mention the time left and ask if there is any need for clarification. Transitions happen with more ease if named. This is not the time to ask new questions.

It's helpful to give the seeker a summary of the highlights with attention to those steps of action that surfaced, if possible. The blessing and honoring of the session will close cosmic doors well.

In the first principle of Grounding, the Moon/Sun Welcome ritual and the Throne Welcome ritual help the seeker enter sacred space. Both assist in closing the reading as well. If you have used one of these two grounding rituals to open the session, choose the same one now for closure. Fan out the cards in front of the seeker so that they may choose one final card as their final gesture.

Moon/Sun Closure Ritual

"Close your eyes. Go back to the beautiful space where you began this session. * Some things have changed during the reading. * The Divine Allies and

Beloved Ancestors have created a circle around you. They bless your endeavors. Allow yourself to receive. * [Now name some of the strongest insights that were mentioned in the reading as if they have already manifested. For example: during the reading, their mother's options of selling her home were discussed. At this point of closure, you could mention that, "You see your mom at peace with making the decision to sell her family home. She is surrounded by loving people."] * The light that was everywhere has moved into one continuous and powerful spiral about two feet from your body. * The spiral attracts the people and experiences you need in your life. It repels all negative influences. * Open your eyes. Please choose one card as a message from your future self. This card is their message to you."

THRONE CLOSURE RITUAL

"Close your eyes. Go back to the throne. * Some things have changed during the reading. * The Divine Allies and Beloved Ancestors have created a circle around you. They bless your endeavors. Allow yourself to receive. * [Now name some of the strongest insights that were mentioned in the reading as if they have already manifested. For example: during the reading, their work pressures were discussed. At this point of closure you could mention that, "You see your boss and colleagues respecting and supporting you."] * [Mention some items from tarot that stood out during the session. For example: You now notice a sword by your right foot. By your left foot is a chalice. Know that these are your power and magic.] * Open your eyes. Please choose one card as a message from your future self, three years from now. This card is their message to you."

Integration—The Sixth Principle

As important as Closure is for both the seeker and the reader, the step of Integration brings the entire reading to a new level. What will the seeker do with this new information? Is there one action step that comes to mind for them? Brainstorming ways to incorporate the messages helps to empower them to act. The insights received once sacred space is opened will return to the ether if not acted on. While this dialogue could take place before closure, processing the reading once it is complete can act as a healthy transition from the sacred space to everyday life.

Helping the seeker visualize the insights, suggesting that they are safe and loved by their Divine Allies and Beloved Ancestors, and finding ways for the reading to become truly alive are potent skills. Readings clarify seeds for change.

Summary

This chapter offers spreads and ideas to create one's own methodology in reading for others. Divination is a very special form of communication. The importance of being free of your own biases as in the Bias-Free spread and keeping your energy protected in the Zip It ritual create necessary boundaries. The six principles of Grounding, Intent, Form, Synchronicity, Closure, and Integration provide a strong structure for reading for others. These principles can be a structure to lean into as you create your own format as a reader. Shifting the dynamics of a seeker's life for the better is the exact reason one would read for another.

Chapter Seven

CALENDAR RITUALS

This chapter explores rituals within a framework of time and the natural forces of light and dark. Daily, monthly, seasonal, and yearly rituals offer powerful rhythms that connects us to nature. The Sunday Grid ritual revolves around the energy flow of the week, while the Moon ritual is a reflection of the month. Birthday rituals mark the passage of one year and offer tools to gather insights from reviewing the past year and looking ahead. The Wheel of the Year is a template for reflecting on the shifting dance between light and dark, the changing of seasons, the passage of time, and other meaningful cycles found in our lives, including times of celebration.

Time is one of our finest natural resources. Sacred time is the inclusion of the past, present, and future. This sense of time is circular or whole, rather than a linear progression.

Rituals mark significant times in our lives such as birth, death, and other major transitions. Aligning with the movement of the calendar and the seasons sets a stage for organic rhythms that connect us to something larger than ourselves. Rituals organize time itself. They are a powerful gesture of enhancing the quality of our own reality.

Seasonal rituals are commonly known as holidays. Holidays are holy days and they act as collective road posts of human timelines within greater rhythms. Including the day before and after a holy day, such as a birthday or a seasonal turning point, enhances the overall rhythm. Holidays or vacations are experiences of time as nonlinear. This break from a regular schedule can provide a deep connection with nature.

The Hierophant, the fifth major arcana, is the tarot representative of ritual. This archetype is often depicted as the pope who sits on a throne in a church. His right hand is raised as a sign of blessing. Two acolytes kneel before him. The Hierophant represents light by building power through cyclic rituals. Repetition creates a certain power all its own. Weekly worship services have been a major ritual for religions. Sunday is often a culmination of looking over the last week and preparing for the new one. There is great wisdom in engaging with the inventory of the past and setting goals for the future. The next ritual is an innovative approach in creating a weekly reset button.

Sunday Grid Ritual

Dedicate a deck solely for this ritual. I use a Marseilles deck. Its minor arcana are brightly colored and numbered pips—the forty cards that range from ace to ten for each of the four suits. The simple numerical pattern is very appealing. Any deck that is highly symbolic or abstract is suitable for this ritual. The cards chosen will not be interpreted but rather hold a visual space much like an altar. They act as a grid by creating a link between all the selected cards.

This grid serves as an energetic boundary for the upcoming week. The first step is to determine certain areas of your living space to be on the grid. For example, I have a second-floor office for clients in my home. Energy flows strongly from clients entering my home. The energy pathway continues up the stairs to my office. I include my work space on the first floor, which is next to the kitchen. The kitchen is another space that's represented on my grid because it is located between my work area and the stairs leading to the office. Finally, my front door is included on the grid.

Once created, the grid itself does not change. New cards are chosen every Sunday. Each card represents an energy for that part of your home. All the cards together are a visual map of how energy will flow through the week.

Every Sunday I gather the cards from last week. I shuffle the deck and ask the Creative Unknown for knowledge about the week to come. I randomly choose four cards. I place the first card in my second-floor office. This card tends to represent an important theme for a few clients that week. The second card is placed at my work station as motivation needed to accomplish tasks. The third card is placed by the fridge and gives insight into nurturing myself and my family. The fourth card is placed near the front door. This tends to be a message of the outside world.

The Sunday Grid ritual is useful for understanding how energy flows through your living space. The chosen cards fortify those areas energetically. This ritual is worth the effort—it provides visual reminders of the flow of spirit-led energy and support during the week.

The Moon Ritual

Let us now look at a monthly cycle, the moon cycle, roughly twenty-eight days that consists of the new moon phase where the moon is waxing, the mid-cycle full moon, and then the waning moon phase. A simple ritual is choosing a card to be placed on the altar for the duration of the moon cycle. An ideal time to choose this card is on the new moon. This card will give insights into the inherent theme of this lunar cycle. A moon ritual that goes a bit more in depth, however, is one that reflects its various phases.

The results you want depend on clear intention and focus. Take some time to consider what you want or need to experience during the upcoming moon cycle. This intention could simply be a state of being or a completion of a certain project. Express desires, needs, or wishes it would fulfill. Each phase of the moon will have its own card suggestions. All of these chosen cards culminate in an overview spread for the entire moon cycle.

The moon goes through various astrological signs through a twenty-eight-day cycle. A little research could be helpful in knowing these influences. In addition to the planetary aspects, the various moons of the year have collected cultural identities. Some examples of these titles may spark a way to frame your intention. Please note that within the Algonquin moon titles, some months have different names from the many different tribes/groups of the Algonquin people.

Moon Names

Month	Algonquin	Celtic	Chinese
January	Wolf	Quiet	Holiday
February	Snow	Ice	Budding
March	Sap	Winds	Sleeping
April	Seed	Growing	Peony
May	Flower	Bright	Dragon
June	Strawberry	Horse	Lotus
July	Buck	Calming	Hungry Ghost
August	Sturgeon	Dispute	Harvest
September	Corn	Singing	Chrysanthe-mum
October	Raven	Harvest	Kindly
November	Hunter's	Dark	White
December	Cold	Cold	Bitter

New Moon—Intention

New moons are an ideal time to initiate divination tools such as a tarot deck. Create your own spell, poem, or blessing. Other creative ways to use the energy of the new moon is by capturing the energy of it by placing a full water bottle overnight in the moonlight.

To create a personal intention for the moon cycle, meditate during the new moon. Visualize what you would love to see or experience by the end of the twenty-eight-day cycle. Dreaming on the night of the new moon may yield messages for the cycle. Whether you choose meditation or dream time, randomly choose one major arcana card that is a response from the Creative Unknown. What is the most vital theme or influence of this month?

First Quarter Moon—Inventory

This phase speaks to the inventory and steps of action that may be needed. How is your intention growing or shifting? How do you need to step up as a co-creator in this process? Randomly pull two cards from the minor arcana. Cups may indicate an emotional reset or vision correction. Wands could call for stronger forms of expression or passion. Pentacles could speak to needed resources. Swords represent effective focus and communication.

Full Moon—Illumination

Things are coming into the light. The essence of your intention and its fruition are fully illuminated now. During the night of the full moon, place the entire tarot deck facedown in a circle around you. Envision rays of light from the moon as if entering through the crown of your head. Moonlight fills your body fully and then permeates the entire space. The changes needed are here and now. Allow all fantasies and wishes to fall away. Accept the response from the Creative Unknown.

As with any work with tarot, pay attention to messages you receive before and during the actual selection of the card. Sensing all the energy when handling the cards can reveal information about the card or the bigger message. For example, while shuffling, you sense a heaviness in your heart. Don't disregard that initial sensation no matter how cheerful you might find the card. Pay special attention to any major arcana because they provide additional resources. Court cards might signify influences, collaborators, or unrecognized support in your endeavor.

From the circle of cards, select three that speak to:

Card One—Releasing: This card illustrates a necessary surrender. It may speak directly to your resistance, illusions, or attachments regarding your intention.

Card Two—Acceptance: What needs to be truly acknowledged at this point? This card's message is what may be required for you to be fully present.

Card Three—Response: As a co-creator, what do you need to allow or receive from the Creative Unknown? The image will deliver a message of the manifestation itself.

Last Quarter Moon—Acceptance

In your meditations, recognize what has been given. With gratitude, choose one card to reflect on the gift, secret, or challenge of the intention.

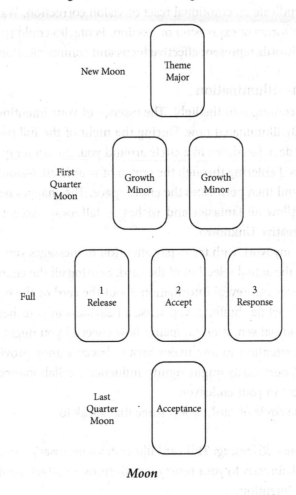

Moon

Before the next dark moon (shortly before the new moon), place all the chosen cards into the moon spread. Allow this full picture to yield additional insights. What picture arises from your intention and the Creative Unknown's response?

Now, let us move on to yearly rituals. An annual event that deserves spiritual recognition is one's birthday. The start of a brand-new birth year opens veils for the year to come. Consider either the Birthday Spiral ritual or the Birthday Council ritual for yourself as well as for others.

The Birthday Spiral ritual is for the day before, on, or after your birthday. It can also make a great birthday gift if done for a friend. In addition to the ritual, pay attention to any common theme of birthday cards and presents. They may foreshadow the year to come.

The following journey prepares a framework for the Birthday Spiral spread. If you record the guided meditation, use the * as pauses. If offered as a gift, read the meditation aloud for the birthday recipient as they lie or sit with their eyes closed. After the guided meditation, you will choose cards for its spread. Gail Fairfield's original spread with one major and one minor card inspired this variation. Separate the deck into two groups, the major and the minor arcana.

Birthday Spiral Ritual

Open the quarters as described in Calling the Circle (pg 17). Light a single candle for the center. Sink into a comfortable pose in the center sitting space.

The Journey

"I stand in a lush landscape. It is my birthday. * I feel safe, loved, and seen. I strongly feel the presence of the Creative Unknown. * I notice one candle burning brightly by my feet. * Other candles start to appear in a spiral. They are birthday candles lit from the year before. * Eventually every year of candles add onto the spiral. * They form a growing spiral around me. * It grows large as the lights honor every year of my life. * Candles of all sizes and shapes of my last incarnation now appear. * Eventually the candles of all of my incarnations join this spiral. It becomes endless. I cannot see the end. * The spiral evolves into one huge light. I am nearly floating from this beautiful representation of my life and lives."

Open your eyes and focus on the single candle flame. Carefully shuffle each group of the major and minor arcana as you recall the significant highlights of this life. For each decade, choose one major arcana and minor arcana card. The major arcana speaks to the "what" as the major reflection of that time. For example, choosing the Star may indicate a time of hope, faith, and self-acceptance. The minor arcana speaks to the "how" as the divine process. For example, choosing the Seven of Swords may show a time when you felt betrayed or let down by a certain group of friends. Because of the loss of trust, you went within and started truly trusting yourself. What did you consider the greatest theme? How did you experience its lessons?

You will now choose the spread's final three cards. They portray insights of the upcoming year. Shuffle all the remaining cards together. The three cards represent the essence, the challenge, and the surprise. Incorporate anything that may have been felt or sensed while shuffling and choosing the cards.

Close your eyes to envision standing again in the center of that powerful spiral of light. Give thanks to the Creative Unknown as you close the quarters.

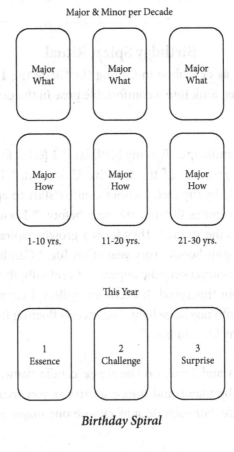

Birthday Spiral

Birthday Council Ritual

This Birthday Council ritual happens over a period of a year. It involves a strong relationship with six cards through this birthday into the next. This spread acts more as a divine committee (pg 96), providing guiding influences through the year.

Decks that are particularly potent for this ritual are ones that represent your cosmology or understanding of the Creative Unknown. Decks such as the Dark Goddess Tarot, the New Mythic Tarot, Pagan Otherworlds Tarot, or the Haindl Tarot present worlds of specific spiritual perspectives. Decide which deck best aligns with your pantheon or spiritual culture for this annual ritual.

Six cards will be chosen on or near your birthday for this first round of the spread. The same cards are revisited at every turning point of the seasons. (These turning points are described fully on pg 138). The six cards represent the four directions, the center, and your year card. Tracking each reading in one journal is recommended for easy recognition of how things progress. Determine the ritual space, consider using the same space for all turning points. Outdoor places such as near a body of water are highly conducive.

The year card, a major arcana that spans the year starting with your birthday, is determined by a simple mathematical formula. Add the numbers of the day and month of your birth with the current year, then reduce these numbers to their lowest total, stopping when you get a number from 1 to 22. The number you calculate correlates to a major arcana that will serve as a major theme for the entire year that commences on your birthday. As an example, if you were born on November 24, add 11 + 24 + 2020 (current year). The total is 2055. Reduce these numbers: 2+0+5+5 = 12. The corresponding major arcana for 12 is the Hanged Man. With the Hanged Man, major themes until your next birthday may include surrender of ego, new perspectives, or a sense of being suspended. If you get a two-digit value of 23 or greater, then add those two together for your total (e.g., for 23, 2+3 = 5). The exception to this formula is a sum of 22. In that case, the corresponding major arcana will be the Fool, which is normally zero, a number that will never be the sum of this calculation.

On the day of your birthday or near it, sort all other cards into their specific suits. Place the groups in the center before beginning the ritual.

Face the east. Imagine your mind being as open as the sky. Allow the power of the upcoming year to make itself known. Receive any image, message, or presence. Record these downloads. Write only as much as needed for recollection later. Face the east again with the sword suit in hand. Randomly choose the facedown card that resonates strongly with the power felt. Lay it facedown in the east.

Face the south. Imagine your creativity and passion burning brightly. Allow the creative force of the upcoming year to make itself known. Receive any image, message, or presence. Record these downloads. Face the south with the wand suit in hand. Choose the card that resonates strongly with the creativity or passion felt. Lay it facedown in the south.

Face the west. Imagine feeling as wide and as deep as an ocean. Allow the vision of the upcoming year to make itself known. Receive any image, message or presence. Record any of these downloads. Face the west with the cup suit in hand. Choose the card that resonates strongly with the energy felt. Lay it facedown in the west.

Face the north. Imagine your body as strong and rooted as a tree. Allow the potential of your resources such as focus, energy, health, wealth, and time of the upcoming year to make itself known. Receive any image, message, or presence. Record these downloads. Face the north with the pentacle suit in hand. Choose the card that resonates strongly with the energy felt. Lay it facedown in the north.

Stand in the center. Imagine that you are connected from above and below. Allow a full sense of your growth in the upcoming year to make itself known. Receive any image, message, or presence. Record these downloads. Shuffle all remaining cards. Randomly choose the card that resonates strongly with the energy felt. Lay it facedown in the center.

Gather and flip over all the chosen cards and the year card. Interpret and record any messages. This first reading of these cards show the potential of the upcoming year.

For each of the seasonal changes, use these original six cards chosen on your birthday. You can use the Celtic Wheel of the Year or a wheel of the year or cycle of seasons that best represents the turning points of your corner of the world and cosmology. For the purposes here, the Celtic Wheel of the Year is the basic template. The messages of the original six cards will evolve over time in surprising ways through the seasons.

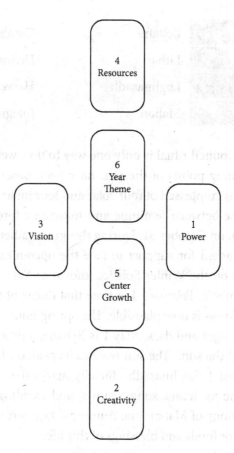

Birthday Council

In each ritual, you will face each direction and take your place in the center to receive the current season's insights or blessings. The spread is a valuable reconnection point between your life and the life force of Earth. The combination of tarot with organic cycles becomes a deeply informative spiritual practice.

Celtic Wheel of the Year

Oct 31	Samhain	Death
Dec 20–22	Yule	Birth
February 2	Imbolc	Purification
March 20–23	Ostara	Growth

May 1	Beltane	Conception
June 20-23	Litha	Divinity
August 1	Lughnasadh	Harvest
September 20–23	Mabon	Integration

The Birthday Council ritual is only one way to flow well with these earth rhythms. The turning points of the year have been observed for centuries. The Celtic Wheel is comprised of four solar and four lunar holy days. It symbolizes the balance between feminine and masculine forces. The new year begins at Samhain, on October 31. During this great gathering, our ancestors are honored and asked for support to face the upcoming winter. The new solar cycle begins on the Winter Solstice known as Yule. The sun grows in potency during Imbolc, February 1, a time that dormant trees begin to stir. Surviving the darkness is now plausible. The Spring Equinox of Ostara resets the balance of the light and dark. May 1 is Beltane, a time for the great love affair of Earth and the sun. The sun reaches its peak on Litha, the Summer Solstice. On August 1, Lughnasadh officially marks the first harvest, originally a Gaelic time for feasts, songs, games, and weddings. The end of the wheel is the ceremony of Mabon, the Autumnal Equinox around September 21, thanksgiving for foods and blessings of this life.

Wheel of the Year

As with the major arcana, each of the turning points are powerful portals. This portal is three days in length: the day before the holy day, the holy day itself, and the day after. They are powerful times for insights for the entire season. These rituals are easily adapted and enjoyed with others. Consider doing the ritual the evening before the actual holy day. Feast afterward, since sharing food is an excellent way to ground after sacred work. The Wheel of the Year template includes:

- *The turning point and its dates:* General times are given but consult with resources for exact dates.

- *Significance and themes:* Keep in mind that these are based on the Gaelic perspective of the seasons.
- *Tarot card associations:* The selection of cards to use is one possible option since the usage of tarot is highly subjective. With time, you will choose your own cards to enhance insights for the ritual.
- *Preparation for the journey*
- *Calling the Circle ritual:* (pg 17) The foundation for the eight rituals within the Wheel of the Year. Decorate the quarter altars to honor the season. These could include fruits, vegetables, flowers, leaves, Halloween candy, pinecones, or scents such as balsam or lavender.
- *Journey:* The journeys of each turning point are the heartbeat of the ritual. They differ from the journeys of the 22 Acts of Magic (pg 42) in that those journeys were vehicles for finding a true intention for the ritual. All journeys take place in the center of the ritual space. Have a journal, soundtrack, and timer nearby if preferred.

Samhain

SAMHAIN TIME AND TITLE

October 31

Summer's End, Celtic New Year, Halloween, Devil's Night

SAMHAIN THEMES

Samhain is the final harvest. It evokes the oncoming winter and the need to prepare for the dark time of the year. Historically it is a bonfire festival that celebrates our ancient community, the Beloved Ancestors. The world slips into the growing darkness. As the Celtic New Year, it is time to make amends and do inventory and divination. Some theme questions might include:

What needs to die?

What fears keep you from feeling love?

What deep secrets will you learn?

SAMHAIN TAROT

The pentacles suit, the Devil, Judgement, Death, and the High Priestess cards

SAMHAIN PREPARATION

Gather photos or mementos of loved ones who have passed. If you have a sense of your blood lineages, include some visuals of their homeland such as a map, foods, or herbs of that region.

Take inventory after a brisk walk or a period of stillness by creating a list of gratitude and a list of current concerns. Within the pros and cons of these lists, craft an intention for insight, blessing, and protection of entering dark times. The Devil, Judgement, Death, and High Priestess cards may provide a fuller intention. Use the Power of Pretend to imagine each of these major arcana as advisors looking over your first draft of the intention. For example, you may craft the intention, "To respect and listen to my body," after noticing a number of concerns regarding your body. Once you have created the intention, say it out loud with each of the selected "advisors." The intention "to respect and listen to my body" may have felt very different in the audience of the Devil compared to that of the High Priestess. Certain feelings of sensuality may have surfaced. You realize that you want to feel sensual again. The intention evolves into, "To respect the sensual power of my body."

Prepare the ritual space through your own sense of this season. You could place a candle, a plate of food, and a glass of a choice beverage for your Beloved Ancestors at each quarter. Separate the cards into two groups: the major arcana and the pentacles suit. The rest of the deck is not needed. Place the two groups of cards and both lists within reach of the center space. Consider recording the meditative section of the journey beforehand to experience it fully during the ritual.

SAMHAIN RITUAL

Stand still for a few minutes. Allow all of your current feelings, thoughts, and sensations to subside. Light a bundle of seasonal herbs. Fan the smoke but do not blow on it. Use the smoke as if you are washing with water, cupping your hands to direct the smoke to your eyes, ears, and heart. Allow the smoke to dissipate any energy that prevents from hearing, seeing, or feeling with love.

Slowly walk clockwise with the herb bundle around the circle starting in the east. Envision walking between columns of the Beloved Ancestors and loved ones who have passed. Bless their presence. At each quarter, call for the wisdom and protection of guardians of the four elemental worlds—water, earth, air, and fire. Welcome them when you sense a shift in energy. Once in the center, speak your intention out loud. Visualize the intention as if it was fully realized. Take a seat for the journey. Recite the following, pausing briefly at each *.

SAMHAIN JOURNEY

"I awake standing in a barren field. * The wind blows through me. It is growing dark yet I have crystal clear vision. * I walk across the field and sense the earth falling asleep under my feet. * Ahead is a circle of massive gray stones with a great tree in the center. It releases its leaves to the wind. * I enter the circle and go near the tree. There is an image of the sun elaborately etched on its bark. * I rest my hand on it and sense the heat of the summer sun within my belly. * As my inner fire grows, I feel the presence of all who love me known or unknown from the other side of the veil. * The sun on the bark changes and shapeshifts, becoming a doorway. I enter the tree through this magical door. * There is a spiral path leading downward to the under-world. * I feel a coolness and power of roots everywhere. * I come to a space that is lit by a multitude of candles. * I sense the presence of a Divine Ally. [Pull one card from the major arcana group.] * The card I chose is this Divine Ally's calling card. They appear in front of me. * We recognize each other. * They gesture for me to take a seat in the middle of this cavern of lights. They ask me to read both the gratitude and concern lists. * I hear my voice fill this holy space. * They ask me to speak the intention out loud three times. * They transform the energy of each recitation. * This Divine Ally responds to my blessings and my fears. I sit quietly and listen as they share an insight of my gifts and challenges. * They ask me to shuffle the pentacles suit and choose seven cards while keeping the sequence of the selection. * I am told that the chosen pentacle cards will serve as a map. The cards in their sequence will define a process for my part in co-creating this intention during this dark time. * The Divine Ally gives me a parting gesture. * I leave this beautiful space to return to the tree's doorway. * As I step out of the tree, I see my beloved friends, family members, and pets from the other side. They are all sitting around a blazing fire. * I join them. We dream together again."

Breathe. Eventually become aware of your current surroundings. Using Calling the Circle as a guide, thank and release each of the four directions starting with north and moving counterclockwise.

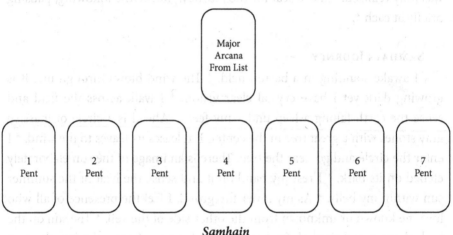

Samhain

After the ritual, bring any drink and foods for ancestors outdoors if possible. Study the pattern of the chosen pentacle cards as a process for this season. Create a way to honor the major arcana that will act as your guide until the next turning point.

Yule

YULE TIME AND TITLE

December 20–22

Christmas, Winter Solstice, Saturnalia, Hanukkah

YULE THEMES

Yule is a Norse word for "wheel." This is the longest night of the year. The birth of the new light is celebrated in many variations.

Some theme questions might be:

What needs to surface?

How can I find stillness with peace?

What idea is being born?

YULE TAROT
The Hermit, the Sun, the Star, and the swords suit

YULE PREPARATION
Prepare the quarters with potent reminders of the season such as balsam, cedar, and mistletoe. Consider creating a small wreath with one candle for the center.

Look over the year up to this point. Record the highlights and challenges of each month. Create another list for wishes and desires of the upcoming year.

Shuffle the swords suit. Choose one facedown card for each of the past eleven months as you focus on the highs and lows of each month. Place the chosen sword cards faceup starting in the east with the month of January. Lay all the month cards in a spiral ending in the center.

Randomly choose one of the three major arcana (the Hermit, the Sun, or the Star) to represent the still point of this ritual. Place all three of these major arcana in the center with this still point card being the only one faceup. Place your wish list near the major arcana. Carry with you the list of highlights and challenges of the months.

YULE RITUAL
Open the quarters. Stop at each of the cards chosen for each month starting with last January. Absorb the image on the card for a few minutes before reading the highs and lows of that month from your list. Reflect again on the card for additional insights needed to honor and release those lessons. This walk through the year eventually ends at December in the center. Sit quietly for a few minutes and light the center candle. The journey can begin.

YULE JOURNEY
"I awake standing at the edge of a forest. * It is dark and the stars are many and bright. The moon shines enough for me to detect a path to walk. *

I am led to a rocky terrain exposing a number of openings of caves. * I enter one cave that seems to call to me. * I enter complete darkness. I sense my way to a place deeper inside. There is one lit candle. I sit down near it and take in the rich stillness. * I become aware of images that seemingly dance on the cave walls. * They are stories of light overcoming darkness. * I close my eyes and see the stories of love overwhelming fear in my lifetime. * Without opening my eyes, I am aware of another presence in the cave with me. * It is a holy being. I open my eyes to see the major arcana chosen as the still point. * We sit together in silence as the light of the candle flickers wildly at times. * I receive communication from this spirit. * They motion for me to read the wishes of the year to come. * As I read, some wishes cause the candle's light to expand or lengthen. * The Divine Ally speaks of these wishes as they progress right now. I feel as if I am hearing my own future script. I am able to see glimmers of this vision. * They quietly disappear after a gesture of farewell. * [Choose one of the two remaining major arcana.] * Feeling hopeful of the year to come, I see another presence enter the cave. This Divine Ally holds the energy of the new year to come. * I remain seated as they add new stories on the cave walls with a wave of their arm. I see new possibilities for myself and those I love. * They direct my attention to one of the wishes in particular. I take it to heart. * They give me a parting gesture before leaving. * As I start to depart myself, I look back. The candle has become a gold orb. It fully illuminates the drawings on the wall. I see a glimmer of a story of my life that seems too fantastical to believe. * The essence of the last Divine Ally will hold the story for me until I can reach that part of the script for myself. * I leave the cave and make my way back to the point where I started. * I feel connected not only to all the stars and trees but to all beings."

Breathe and slowly return to center. Pick up all the sword cards that represented the past months. Be intentional gathering up the past to make way for the new. Close the quarters with gratitude.

If possible, sit by a fire or by one candle. Allow the darkness of the past year to be illuminated by a new light. End the evening by asking the guardian of the new year for a dream of insight of the upcoming year.

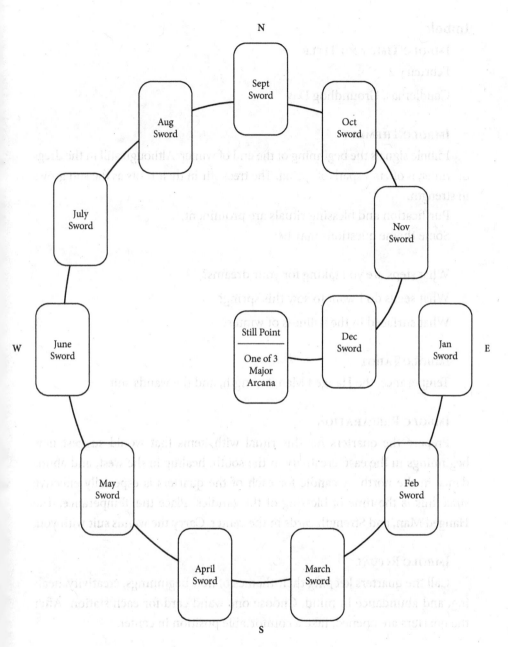

N

Sept
Sword

Aug
Sword

Oct
Sword

July
Sword

Nov
Sword

W   June
Sword

Still Point

One of 3
Major
Arcana

Dec
Sword

Jan
Sword   E

May
Sword

Feb
Sword

April
Sword

March
Sword

S

Yule

Imbolc

Imbolc Time and Title
February 2

Candlemas, Groundhog Day

Imbolc Themes
Imbolc signals the beginning of the end of winter. Although still in the dregs of winter, it offers a spark of spring. The trees stir in their roots as the sun grows in strength.

Purification and blessing rituals are prominent.

Some theme questions may be:

What steps are you taking for your dreams?

What seeds do I want to sow this spring?

What surfaced in the stillness of winter?

Imbolc Tarot
Temperance, the Hanged Man, Strength, and the wands suit

Imbolc Preparation
Prepare the quarters for this ritual with items that would suggest new beginnings in the east, creativity in the south, healing in the west, and abundance in the north. A candle for each of the quarters is especially effective since this is the time of blessing of the candles. Place the Temperance, The Hanged Man, and Strength cards in the center. Carry the wands suit with you.

Imbolc Ritual
Call the quarters keeping their themes of new beginnings, creativity, healing, and abundance in mind. Choose one wand card for each station. After the quarters are opened, take a comfortable position in center.

IMBOLC JOURNEY

"I stand at the beginning of a labyrinth. * I can't see the center but trust that I will be led there. * As I follow the various twists and turns, the scenery evolves into a fantastic landscape of evocative statues and hedges. * I let go of control to enjoy the discoveries and symbols along the way. * [Choose one of the three major arcana cards.] * The chosen Divine Ally makes itself known to me. * They join me. * I am comforted by their support as I feel the last wave of the darkness and heaviness of the winter. They communicate about the safekeeping of my well-being, especially the boundaries needed currently. * We eventually come to a place to rest. * I thank them. They slip into liminal space. * [Choose a major arcana card from the remaining two.] * The second Divine Ally approaches. * I need to adjust to their energy because I feel all the potential of my life in their presence. * We continue the path of the labyrinth. * The path becomes one of many lights. * The Divine Ally communicates about the ways that I add light in this world. * In the distance I can see the center. The third Divine Ally is waiting for me there. * With that sighting of the new guide, my current companion disappears. * I make my way to center with a renewed sense of being loved. * The path pours into this central point. The entire area has an electric charge as I step into it. * I take my place next to this third Divine Ally. * A wave of healing energy rises up through my feet. The energy is being directed by the Divine Ally. * I feel a new self within, vulnerable yet invincible. * A sense of calm confidence fills me. * This Divine Ally communicates how this new self will appear in the world. * They place the remaining wands suit in my hands as they depart. * I too leave this magnificent center to return to the starting point. * Some of these wands will speak to the process I will need for the rest of the year. * I choose wand cards along the way whenever I feel the impulse, keeping the order of the sequence of the selection."

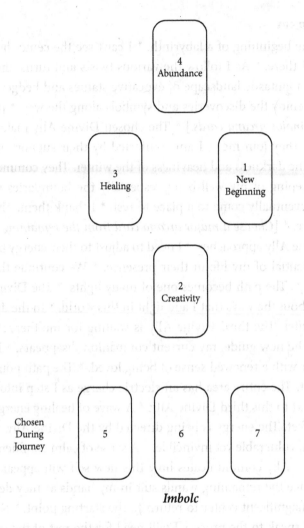

Slowly breathe to return to the current center. Lay out the wands in the order they were chosen. For example, the cards chosen for the quarters are:

- Ace of Wands as the new beginnings in the east
- Knight of Wands as my creativity in the south
- Six of Wands shows the healing in the west
- Three of Wands is the abundance in the north

The ace is a potent symbol of a new sense of identity. There is a great deal of vitality for creativity as shown in the Knight of Wands. The Six of Wands shows important day-to-day decisions for healing. One may need to wait but there is abundance on its way as reflected in the Three of Wands.

Let us say that during the journey, three wand cards are chosen. The sequence is the Five of Wands, Two of Wands, and Queen of Wands. The cards chosen on impulse show a process that is rocky at times but ultimately results in a strong sense of creative vision and power. This wave of energy may easily be the one for the rest of the year.

In a counterclockwise direction, thank and release the guardians for the quarters. Nurture yourself in some manner, perhaps a hot bath with Epsom salts or a cup of hot chocolate.

Ostara

Ostara Time and Title

March 20–23

Spring Equinox

Ostara Themes

Ostara is the first equinox of the year. It is equal parts light and dark, day and night. This ritual honors the rise of a new spring with respect to resurrection or as a phoenix from its ashes.

Some theme questions may be:

How do you wish to feel new?

What ideas or relationships are starting to grow in new ways?

Ostara Tarot

The Fool, Judgement, and all the minor arcana

Ostara Preparation

In this ritual, one raw egg will be destroyed and one hard-boiled egg will be eaten. Depending on your ability to do so, the raw egg will be deliberately tossed outside into a garden or soil to be taken up by earth. If this is not feasible, smashing the egg in a bowl will suffice. The hard-boiled egg (or a creative alternative such as a chocolate egg) should be prepared to eat during the ritual.

Organize the tarot deck into three groups. First, keep only the Fool and Judgement cards from the major arcana. Second, separate the rest of the minor arcana into three groups: the Light Self, the Dark Self, and all others. This structure is a variation of the Light/Shadow/Dark ritual (pg 103). Define "light" and "dark" by your own understanding. Any cards that have no charge either way can go into a toss group.

Prepare the quarters using spring symbols such as seedlings, flowers, etc. Place the Fool and Judgement cards and the light and dark groups at the center. Set the raw egg (with bowl if necessary), hard-boiled egg, and a marker in center as well.

Ostara Ritual

Call in the quarters after you have done some form of grounding for yourself. Take your place in the center.

Take a few minutes to consider the Judgement card's message of an authentic self surfacing. Shuffle the Dark Self group of cards. Focus on current imbalances or chronic patterns. Choose one card. Within one or two words, describe the essence of this card as it pertains to what needs to be released in order for true integration to happen. Use your marker to print these words onto the shell of the raw egg.

Whether you throw this egg outside or in a bowl, hold it. Focus on the imbalance and the way it impedes your life, start to roll the egg around in your hand. Eventually feel the yolk of the egg gain weight as if it is absorbing the negative consequences. Send all thoughts or unwanted energies into the yolk as you continue to swirl the egg. Allow the energy of frustration to build up within you as if this one aspect totally consumes your life. Let it build to a pressure point both within yourself and the yolk. When ready, release the egg and the energy by throwing the egg with all your might onto a patch of ground or into the bowl. Imagine a release of this pattern with this gesture.

Reset in the center. Gently shift your focus to the Fool card. Closely inspect its details. As you shuffle and choose one card within the Light Self group, imagine taking on the Fool's movement toward the best version of yourself. Choose three cards that will signify the next right steps toward this destiny. Look at the three cards for any pattern or states of being that would be helpful. Place your hand a few inches above the hard-boiled egg. Use the Power of Pretend to transmit the vitality of these three cards into the egg itself. Savor each bite as you eat the egg. Ingest those messages.

Thank and release each of the quarters.

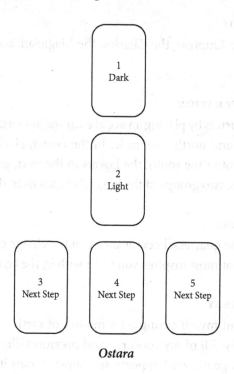

Ostara

Beltane

BELTANE TIME AND TITLE

May 1

Maypole

BELTANE THEMES

Beltane is one of the four fire festivals of the Celtic Wheel. The other three are Imbolc, Lughnasadh, and Samhain. This peak of spring is an honoring of the sacred marriage of the Goddess and the Green Man. Conception and fertility will bring future benefits for all on this planet.

Some theme questions may be:

How committed are you to love?

What hopes and dreams can be enacted?

Do your feminine and masculine aspects support each other?

What is the dance between your visions and manifestations?

BELTANE TAROT

The Lovers, the Empress, the Chariot, the Magician, aces, and kings and queens

BELTANE PREPARATION

Prepare the quarters by placing an ace at each station: east—sword, south—wand, west—cup, and north—pentacle. In the center, place the Magician in the east, the Chariot in the south, the Lovers in the west, and the Empress in the north. Place the two groups of the kings and queens in the center.

BELTANE RITUAL

As you open the quarters, become aware of the charge of each of the aces. Choose the one that most inspires you to sit with in the center.

BELTANE JOURNEY

"I awake to find myself sitting on a mound of earth. * I allow the earth to support me fully. All of my concerns and pressures diminish as I become more present. * A gentle mist appears and slowly wraps itself around me. * I am being shifted to another time and place. * Eventually I sense a landing. My feet touch the ground. The mist dissipates. * I open my eyes to the new surroundings. * The earth feels much younger, more primal. * I am standing in a valley full of flowers. * I lie down in this beauty. * I am intoxicated with the fertile earth underneath me and the bright blue sky above. * The earth opens into a big hole. I float down through the layers of rock and black soil. * As I descend, I am aware of becoming the ace that called to me during the calling of the quarters. * I am the pure energy of this ace. * The only real sense of who I was is my breath. * The Magician appears in the east. * They channel the energies from above and send that as a wave below to me. * The vitality of this wave shapes my very being. I become form. * My essence now has an outer edge. * I enjoy the sensation of feeling and sensing the soil. * The Chariot appears in the south. * They send rays of light from their solar plexus to me. * I feel a sense of movement upward through the soil. * I grow slowly and steadily with the support of The Chariot's will. * I feel at ease as I lengthen upward. * The Lovers manifest in the west. * They send refreshing waters to me. * My growth accelerates in all directions. * I focus only upward and continue to grow stronger and more resilient. * The Empress appears in the north. * They help me break through the surface of earth to feel the sun and sky. * The Empress guides me in bringing my essence of this ace into the world."

Take a few minutes to become fully present in the center. Consider your experience of the growth cycle of the chosen ace.

Shuffle the four queens facedown. Choose one queen in particular. They speak of the needed feminine or yin traits needed for this ace/idea/state of being to come into being. Repeat with the four kings to select the one whose masculine or yang aspects are most needed for growth and manifestation. Consider a sacred marriage of this queen and king. What might be their greatest strength and alchemy as a couple? Sense this union within yourself.

Close the circle in gratitude. Record impressions of your journey and of the queen and king of this Beltane.

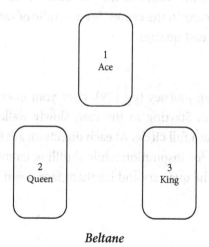

Beltane

Litha

LITHA TIME AND TITLE

June 20–22

Summer Solstice

LITHA THEMES

Litha is the observation of the sun at its peak. We have reached the very top of the wheel. The sun at its full potency impregnates the earth.

Some theme questions may be:

What higher purpose are you willing to lose yourself in?

Who or what do you serve?

What wants to be expressed fully?

LITHA TAROT

The Fool, the Magician, the High Priestess, the World, and the minor arcana

LITHA PREPARATION

Decorate the quarters with various herbs and flowers. Separate the minor arcana into their own suits. Place the swords suit in the east, the wands in the south, the cups in the west, and the pentacles in the north. Place the four mentioned major arcana in the center. Set a bundle of seasonal herbs, lighter, and container at the east quarter.

LITHA RITUAL

As in the Samhain journey (pg 139), clear your energies with the smoke of a bundle of herbs. Starting in the east, slowly walk clockwise with the smoking herbs. Make a full circle. At each direction, ask for the loving guardians of that element for inspiration while shuffling its minor arcana. Choose one card at each of the quarters and lay them face down in the center. Take a seat in the center.

LITHA JOURNEY

"I stand at the edge of a cliff. * I sense complete potential before me. * I am able to step out of the fear and restrictions of my own beliefs. * I take a step into the unknown. * At first, I am surrounded by clouds everywhere, feeling nothing underneath me as I float. * I am being moved as if I was in the currents of a river. * In the distance, a dog barks. * The clouds seem to dissipate as I feel myself being lowered onto a clearing on a plateau. * A small dog waits for me before running ahead onto a path. * My body feels light and loose. * I follow the twists and turns of the path into a grove of trees. * A stone altar stands in the midst of these trees. * On the altar I can see the four minor arcana chosen earlier in the ritual. * I see the potential of something very special in these four cards. * Energy flows through my body as I become aware of the trees and sky around me. * I raise my hand over each one to take in its power. [*Literally do the same with the actual four cards.*] * My hand radiates light. * The cards slowly disappear and in their place appear the four tools themselves, my sword, wand, cup, and pentacle. * I gather them in my bag and continue along the path. * The landscape of trees and greenery slowly evolve into a white desert. * The sands are the remains of what was once a great sea. * Ahead is a temple. I go toward it. * I catch the scent of incense floating near the temple's entrance. * I enter the temple and feel an instant relief from the dry heat. * There is a throne situated between a black and white pillar. * A current as strong as the one in the clouds moves me to take my place on this throne. * The bliss of just being on this throne is combined with the magic of the clouds and the elements of the altar. * A scroll appears in my lap. It is the script of this incarnation that was created before taking this form. * I feel a destiny that is attainable. I am at peace. * I close my eyes and am transported to the edge of the cliff again. * An image of my Destiny Self, the one who completed this incarnation, fully appears in the sky before me. * I step into them."

Take a few minutes to return to this current time and place. Allow additional insights to come from this journey of the Fool on the path, the Magician at the altar, the High Priestess in the desert temple, and from the finale of entering yourself as the cosmic dancer in the World card. Close the four quarters. Take in the long summer night in some form such as a walk.

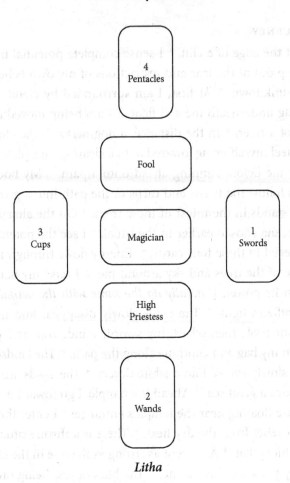

Litha

Lughnasadh

LUGHNASADH TIME AND TITLE

August 1

Lammas

LUGHNASADH THEMES

Lughnasadh is a Gaelic festival that would start at the time of the first grain harvests of the year. The sun as king was considered divine and must die for his strength to be passed into earth for the harvest. People celebrated this time with feasts, marriages, and contests.

Some theme questions might be:

What currently needs action?

How can you fully accept current consequences as a result of your past
choices?

LUGHNASADH TAROT

The Hanged Man, Justice, and the cups

LUGHNASADH PREPARATION

Place an assortment of fruits, breads, nuts, and grape juice or wine at the
four quarters. Shuffle and place the cups cards, the Hanged Man, and Justice
at center.

LUGHNASADH RITUAL

As you open the quarters, take a sip or taste at each station. Take your place
in the center for the journey.

LUGHNASADH JOURNEY

"I sit in the middle of a great field. * I am grateful for everything this
planet provides for me. * I sense the stillness of a warm afternoon. The sound
of birds fills the air. * My thoughts start to flow easily. * I lie on my back.
Drops of rain start to fall on me. A gentle rain begins. * I feel as if I am part
of the land with my thirst also being quenched. * I honor my heart's ability
to love life. * The sun appears again. I hear a symphony of cicadas. I become
fully aware of my body and all that it does for me. * I appreciate the sun and
the heat it provides. * I sit up and take in the last of the summer sun. I am
home here. I am home in myself."

Choose enough cards of the cups suit with the Hanged Man and Justice to
create a fan for yourself. Close your eyes while slowing your breath, thoughts,
and feelings. Fan yourself under the last of this hot sun. What vision might
arise? What needs to happen before the rhythms of fall enter? From the fan,
select three to six cards. Let the story unfold through each of the pictures
as in one of the Story spreads (pg 36). Gather the messages for later reflections as the season progresses. If you received the Hanged Man or the Justice
cards, focus on their themes daily until the coming equinox.

When you feel full, go to each quarter with thanks and a gesture of closing the veils. Offer the quarter foods to outdoor creatures.

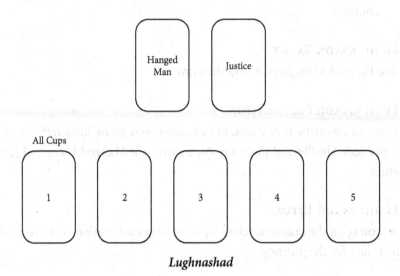

Lughnashad

Mabon

MABON TITLE AND TIME

September 20–23

Autumnal Equinox

MABON THEMES

This equinox marks the last balance of equal light and dark of the year. Finding a neutral point can influence a smooth entrance into the increasing darkness. It is the second harvest and is celebrated through feasts and giving thanks.

Some theme questions might be:

What do you need to hear?

What habits, beliefs, or relationships need to end?

How do you express gratefulness for the people in your life?

MABON TAROT
Death, the Empress, the Moon, the Sun, and the rest of the deck

MABON PREPARATION
Decorate the quarters with candles and autumn essences such as apples, pinecones, leaves, squash, and cider. Place the Sun card at the east, Death at the south, the Moon at the west, and the Empress at the north. Place the rest of the deck facedown in the center.

MABON RITUAL
Open the quarters with the following reflections at each station:

• East: Allow the Sun card to mirror the joy, pleasure, and gifts of this time of year.
• South: Reflect on the Death card regarding losses and challenges.
• West: Focus on the Moon card for the way mystery is moving through your life.
• North: With the energy of the Empress card, give gratitude for all the ways you are blessed and loved.

Make your way to center. The journey is a fifteen-minute meditation of looking inward for the balance of energies. Choose cards during the meditation when you feel the impulse to do so. Lay them facedown and then continue the meditation. These cards will help leverage a stronger sense of your own light and dark aspects. After the meditation, look at the cards chosen as ways to balance your energies. It might help to have one key word for each card; not only is it easier to comprehend, the cards together may comprise one full message.

When ready, close the quarters in gratitude. Savor each bite or sip.

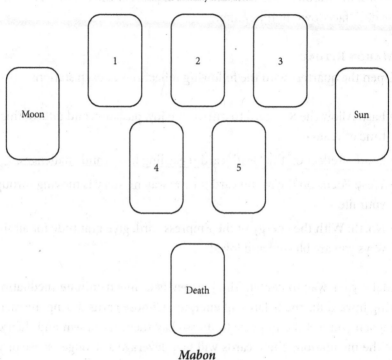

Mabon

Summary

The calendar rituals of this chapter honor the resource of time. The weekly service of the Sunday Grid ritual, the monthly Moon ritual, and the Birthday rituals strengthen a connection to the greater rhythm of the Creative Unknown.

The Wheel of the Year is presented through the framework of the eight Celtic turning points—Samhain, Yule, Imbolc, Ostara, Beltane, Litha, Lughnasadh, and Mabon. Rather than a calendar year, each of these eight rituals reflect the dynamic dance of light and dark. Each holy day is described. Themes and tarot cards related to each turning point are offered for exploration and inspiration for a journey.

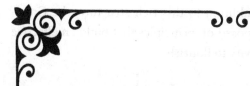

Chapter Eight

GROUP RITUALS

The rituals in this chapter can be used for gatherings of four or more participants including workshops, conferences, meetups, and teambuilding. Unlike the previous chapter that primarily used the Calling the Circle ritual to create a sacred space, these rituals lean more toward educative explorations. The suggestions of movement within the space and time may need to be adapted for your own purposes. Let us begin with suggestions for creating strong group dynamics.

Creating an environment so everyone feels safe to follow their own curiosity requires some key practices. If at all possible, create a circular seating arrangement. An excellent resource for group work that uses the circle as the ultimate structure is the methodology of *The Circle Way: A Leader in Every Chair* by Ann Linnea and Christina Baldwin. Their major tenets of safety, boundaries, and purpose bring groups to new levels of trust. In addition to this rich structure, the Creating the Container template is composed of principles that build an effective environment for your planned activity to flourish.

Creating the Container Template

Opening

Greet everyone as they enter the room.

Introduce yourself and give an outline of the gathering.

Mention essentials such as bathroom locations and break times.

There will be various levels of tarot experience. Be sure to welcome the beginners as well as the seasoned readers. If folks have had no tarot exposure, suggest ideas that allow them to trust the story that they get from the image (versus trying to apply traditional definitions of the cards). Introduce the Power of Pretend to encourage them to trust their imagination in knowing how any chosen card makes them feel.

Confidentiality

Ask participants to raise their hands as a sign of agreement to keep anything discussed by others in complete confidentiality.

Expectations

An important clarification to make is that in a peer group setting, everyone must be responsible for their own well-being. If a person does not want to participate or respond, give them the option to say "pass." Their choice will be respected with no questions asked. If anyone decides not to engage in an activity, ensure they respect those that do by remaining quiet and observing.

Those who feel uneasy speaking in a group setting should be encouraged to speak first. Those who are comfortable speaking their minds can be invited to wait for others to go first. All side conversations are discouraged while others are speaking.

Discourage participants from looking up card definitions in books or on cell phones. This gathering is an exploration of each person's creative authority. There is no right or wrong, only in the moment perspectives.

Check In

Provide each participant with a deck if they do not have one. Have everyone shuffle their deck and choose one card. Instruct those in the circle not to look at their card until it is their turn to check in. Starting with the person to the left of you, go around the circle clockwise. Have each person say their name and a single word to capture their current energy level (tired, excited, relaxed, curious, etc.). Then have them look at the card and describe what its message is or their immediate sense of what wants to surface for them in this gathering.

During the Planned Activity

If needed, gently remind folks of the boundaries that have been set. For instance, you may need to encourage the shy ones to engage or ask all participants to be attentive to timelines.

Feedback

Having a discussion of the activity may elevate the understanding of it. Be clear about the structure of the feedback. For instance, have everyone respond, limiting their verbal feedback to no more than three minutes each. You could also open the floor by asking for only three people to respond if the group is large. Having folks respond popcorn-style (however and whomever) is less rigid and removes the pressure of everyone needing to respond. Encourage the shy folks to join in. Give gentle reminders of time limits.

Closing

Starting with the person to the right of you and moving in a counterclockwise direction, ask two final questions of everyone: What insights would you like to remember from this gathering? How did the initial card's message manifest for you?

When channeled well, group dynamics are powerful. As a skill, it ensures everyone feels validated. (See the previously mentioned circle way, created by Ann Linnea and Christina Baldwin.) If time permits, the Mind Gripe ritual is a bit more elaborate in the setting of trust but worth the effort.

Mind Gripe Ritual

Ideally, the Mind Gripe ritual occurs after the check in but before the main activity. This ritual helps everyone become more present with themselves and therefore with the group. Provide everyone with an index card. Have everyone take three minutes to print five things that their brain is holding onto right now: petty complaints, big concerns, obligations that won't stop nagging them, insecurities, desires, fantasies, or expectations of themselves or this gathering. Some examples could be: *these chairs aren't comfortable; I have to do laundry when I get home; will he be able to move to assisted living?* They should record any thought that is loud or persistent without censoring. If thoughts are about someone else, only pronouns should be used, not formal names. These gripes are going to be dissolved collectively so there is no fear of the individual sharing personal gripes.

After five minutes, collect all the index cards. Shuffle them well. Turn the lights down low and have everyone close their eyes as they imagine the center of the room to be a powerful portal to the Creative Unknown. Have them listen with an open heart to those things that we battle every day. Using the Power of Pretend, suggest that each person send each gripe to the portal in the room to free the writer from its energy. Read at least one gripe from each index card slowly. The energy of the entire group can change during this act of empathy and release.

When done, place the pile of gripe cards in a designated place. Suggest thinking of this portal to reset focus if a person's thoughts start to stray or energy becomes low. After the gathering, discard all the cards. Burning them is satisfying and thorough. They should at least be torn up so that they're unrecognizable.

Icebreaker Ritual

Another ritual that provides a strong sense of connection in a group is the Icebreaker ritual. It serves as a wonderful first exercise, whether the gathering is being held for a few hours or an entire weekend. This ritual supports twelve or more participants. If there are fewer, it can be adapted as a discussion. The cards create a collaborative focus for each participant.

Have everyone take a few minutes to shuffle their deck as they think about their lives lately. Using one deck for all to choose from is an option as well. Have them choose one card to receive an insight about raising the quality of love in their everyday life. Allow them to go anywhere in the space to sit quietly to reflect with this card for five minutes. For those brand new to tarot, encourage them with some of the observation ideas from the Entering the Card ritual (pg 25), such as what thought, memory, message, or idea is being activated within.

After this time, their chosen card becomes their admission ticket to their particular tarot family during the session. For example, if they got the Four of Swords card, they will join the swords suit family. Instruct everyone to find their fellow group members within their tarot family's designated area.

Family	Location in Room	Theme of the Family
Swords Ace–10	East wall	Power
Wands Ace–10	South wall	Ideas
Cups Ace–10	West wall	Vision
Pentacles Ace–10	North wall	Resources
Court Cards	Center of room	Humanity
Major arcana	Find a separate room	Mystery

Once everyone is in place, give them fifteen minutes to agree on one common message between all the individual insights. Initially, the dialogue in each group begins with having each member speak to the messages they received from their own card. The goal is for the small group to discover a unifying message of raising the level of love within the framework of their particular tarot family theme. For example, if everyone in the wands group decided there is a repeating message of conflict and struggle among the cards they have chosen, the proactive and unifying message to raise the level of love within their family of creative expression could be "transform the energy of tension and conflict for better ideas to surface."

Those participants who draw major arcana cards will not need to collaborate or find a common theme with each other. Instead, these group members remain as individuals. They use their fifteen minutes and the Power of Pretend to embody their major arcana to create a unique message about raising the level of love within mystery.

After the fifteen minutes is up, each small group chooses one speaker to deliver their family's message to the collective. Direct everyone to their original seats except the five speakers and the major arcana group. Starting with the swords family, each speaker will deliver the message that gives insight to their respective family themes of power (swords), ideas (wands), vision (cups), resources (pentacles), and humanity (court cards).

For the grand finale, have the speakers stand silently in the circle as each major arcana introduces themselves. In silence, each will walk around the other speakers three times. They then stand in the center to deliver a succinct statement to the entire collective regarding mystery. This message can be delivered in poetic or mythic terms regarding the greater forces of love and guidance that are currently available for the collective. For example, one person chose the High Priestess. After the speakers of the other tarot families have spoken, this high priestess announces their title. They walk slowly around the other speakers and quietly make their way to the center of the circle. They pretend to read from a scroll as they say, "Dear ones, much is hidden from us now, but know that there is great love working behind closed veils. Be patient. All will be revealed in divine time." Any remaining members of the major arcana group will then perform similarly in turn. Encourage those participants without much tarot knowledge to use the Power of Pretend and enjoy the theatrics of assuming this persona. The collective effort of creating messages for the whole group has a strong bonding effect.

Stranger in Town Ritual

Another ritual that can create a strong connection among a group is the Stranger in Town ritual. This ritual asks that readers determine fictional cultures that lead to creating nonfictional results. It needs a minimum of nine participants.

Divide the participants as evenly as possible at tables or in various circles of chairs. Each group collectively decides how they will choose three cards. After the cards are chosen, the groups have fifteen minutes to decide three major values of their fictional "town" (i.e., their table).

Encourage the participants to be creative and lean into science fiction and fantasy. For example, with the lusty and carefree Knight of Wands as a major principle, they could be a people who don't believe in marriage, therefore no one in the town ever marries. The three cards together could also surface a major value as well. For example, a table might have chosen the Ace of Cups, Six of Cups, and Nine of Wands. The love of the Ace of Cups, the innocence of the Six of Cups, and the guarded quality of the Nine of Wands could combine to create the value that in this town all disputes are settled by playing a game.

Assign a participant from each town (table) to go to another town. Use a method in doing so, perhaps the Aries at each table, or the ones wearing green, etc. These select participants will all be considered Exile 1 at the new table. For ten minutes, the exile remains silent while observing the new town folks acting out one of their chosen values. During this demonstration, nothing is explained to the exile. Using the examples above, the town folk could talk about the irrelevance of wearing wedding rings or two of the "citizens" could have an argument and start to play the hand game of pat-a-cake to resolve it.

Assign a second participant from each table, to be known as Exile 2, to join their fellow townsperson Exile 1. For five minutes, the town folk at that table remain silent as Exile 1 informs Exile 2 about how to behave by the new rules. The exiles then both speak about their hometown's culture.

Have everyone return to their original table. Encourage a ten-minute free flow of perceptions from each member about their experiences. At the ritual's completion, feedback with the whole group becomes potent when coming from each table:

1. Exile 1 speaks of their experience before they were joined by their fellow townie.

2. Exile 1 talks about any shift of thought or feeling when joined by Exile 2.

3. One townsperson talks about how they felt while needing to be silent as they listen to the two exiles.

4. Exile 2 speaks to learning about another town.

The Stranger in Town ritual not only supports working collaboratively in interpreting the cards, it also helps people explore how their perceptions may be shaped by others. It is a powerful experience about exiles, a dynamic to elicit much needed awareness from all of us.

Our Story Ritual

Collaboration with readers of various levels of knowledge can produce amazing results. Readers from beginners to seasoned practitioners can enjoy how the Our Story ritual generates many different stories using the same tarot card. This ritual works well with a group or grouping of four to six participants. The leader can join in as a participant.

Inform everyone that one tarot card will surface many stories and memories. Only one card will be selected for the entire group. During this ritual, a gesture will be gathered from each person that comes from natural movements while they tell their story. Each participant will be asked for permission to use one gesture witnessed by the leader. There is no need to perform or overthink anything.

Have one person shuffle a deck and pull a card. This card will be passed to every reader in the circle to surface a personal memory or story. Encourage any story that seems to be triggered whether the connection to the card makes sense or not to the others. Each person will be given three minutes. As the leader, notice any gesture of the first person to speak of their story. This gesture could be as subtle as the tilt of their head, a shoulder shrug, or a wave of their hand. When they are finished, ask their permission to use the gesture. They are in full creative authority of saying no or wanting another gesture to be used. Demonstrate the gesture to the group and have everyone copy the movement.

Have each reader speak of their story. Ask for permission to reflect one gesture as they told their story and then have the group copy it. Be aware, however, that people will become self-conscious once they know their gestures are being observed. Perhaps take a few breaks between readers to have everyone close their eyes, breathe, and let their bodies move without judgment.

Once everyone has told their story, pass the card around again. In this second round, each participant repeats their gesture slowly in silence. The group responds by mirroring this gesture. Do a third round of enacting the gestures together at a medium pace.

Open the floor for feedback. You could ask about how this card evolved as it became increasingly nonverbal. Another topic could be their experience of the personal gestures creating a bigger story for all.

As a language of images, tarot lends itself to opening up memories and associations much like the Rorschach inkblot test. The Our Story ritual contributes to the intimacy of the group through witnessing what is being said by word and gesture. Often the culminating story is a powerful testimony of this single card.

Celtic Cross Ritual

Storytelling is a natural consequence of using the tool of tarot. The Celtic Cross spread, the most traditional spread, is a foundation for a good story. There are variations of the Celtic Cross spread, so choose the one you prefer if the example is not a good fit. A person will represent each position of this spread in the Celtic Cross ritual, so it would help to have at least eleven participants—ten folks for the spread and one as the seeker. The leader can join in as a participant.

Have everyone take a few minutes to create a specific question. If needed, borrow ideas from the Fat Rabbit ritual (pg 119) for relevant and personal questions.

The next step is determining who will be the seeker. As the leader, choose one card. Have everyone choose a card. The person who has a card closest in relationship to the one you picked becomes the seeker. For example, if you chose the Queen of Pentacles, the one participant who chose a pentacle court card becomes the seeker. If no card comes close to your card in terms of suit or position, use your discretion or have everyone draw again.

The seeker states their question out loud. Omitting the seeker's card, a volunteer shuffles and places ten selected cards into the Celtic Cross spread (provide an easy-to-follow diagram for the group). Allow three minutes for everyone to silently look at the spread with the seeker's question in mind. Have each participant choose one of these ten cards and take that position in a standing Celtic Cross spread formation in the room.

1. The situation

2. Influences affecting the situation

3. Deep roots regarding this situation

4. Recent past

5. Seeker's expectation

6. Near future

7. Seeker's attitude

8. Timing or worldly influences

9. Seeker's hope or fear

10. Possible outcome

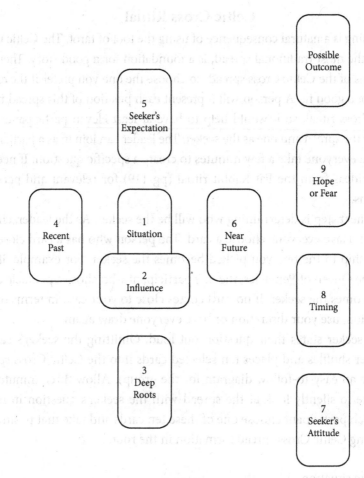

Celtic Cross

The seeker will go to each person in the spread and state their question out loud. Start with the first position and go through the numerical sequence. Each person will start their response by stating their position. The objective is for each person to answer from the perspective of their card and position in the spread. For example, the seeker asks if their hobby could be a small business. The seventh position's card is Three of Pentacles. The person speaking as the Three of Pentacles would say, "I am your attitude. As the Three of Pentacles, I would advise that you take the time to learn as much as possible about starting a small business as you continue to hone your craft."

After the seeker has received insights from all the positions, have everyone return to their original seats. Invite the seeker to share their feedback and what they thought of the reading as a whole. Have others give feedback about their experience or how the reading evolved from their initial viewing of it.

The Celtic Cross spread is the most popular of spreads yet takes time and practice to find its flow. Allowing different voices of the spread to be heard gives the opportunity to build strong reading skills. The Celtic Cross ritual provides a visceral exploration of this thorough and complete spread.

Initial Image Ritual

Sharing stories through one card or role-playing an entire tarot spread can open doors of new perspectives. Another group activity is supporting each other in practicing certain skills of reading. Developing psychic skills requires tangible practice. The Initial Image ritual offers a structure to do just that. While it is easily adapted for partner work, however, the benefits of mutual support and diverse responses when practiced as a group are profound.

The "initial image" is a quickly flashed impression or psychic message before reading any cards. This could be received as a visceral sensation, visual image, short scene, or a sense of "knowing" without explanation. This knowing means that you really don't see anything as much as sense a story that appears in your imagination. It may feel as though you are creating it, but trust that you are *receiving* it. It is useful in seeking the right tone or direction for the effectiveness of the reading's impact for the seeker. In the Initial Image ritual, the group will receive an initial image for the one seeker.

Ask for a volunteer to receive a group reading. Have them take a seat where they are easily viewed by everyone. Have the seeker take a few minutes to formulate a question for themselves. The group can support them via the Fat Rabbit ritual (pg 119) or similar, with the seeker ultimately selecting the question to hold silently.

Have everyone close their eyes as the seeker says their full name three times. Have the group open their eyes. For three minutes, the group will scan the seeker using the Power of Pretend in receiving images, energies, sensations, or messages about the seeker's energy. The seeker keeps their eyes closed and focuses solely on their question.

Invite the seeker to open their eyes and have the readers share their impressions and downloads from the scan. Then ask the seeker to share their question. Each reader randomly chooses one card as a response. Have the readers incorporate all they sensed initially and the chosen card into the answer of the seeker's question.

For example, as the seeker was thinking of their question, a reader received a scene of the seeker as much younger getting mad playing some board game. The seeker asks, "What do I need to know about an upcoming family reunion?" The reader chose the five of wands. The reader answers that competition is a highly charged dynamic within the family, so either don't play games or keep your sense of humor.

The focus of the feedback is on the experience of receiving the initial image. Avoid attempts by the readers to have the seeker validate their answers. Give the seeker full permission to take what they can use and leave the rest.

Chairs Ritual

While reading tarot is an act of receiving information from images and the patterns they form, it is critical to listen to one's intuition in selecting how to perceive and interpret. The Chairs ritual offers a variety of options that are ultimately chosen by one's internal knowing or sense. These internal impulses of your emotional wisdom, physical sensations, mental direction, and your spirit open new worlds of possibilities.

The space greatly determines the flow of this ritual. An ideal space allows for five chairs four feet from each other against a wall with a "lane" of approximately twelve feet extending straight from the front of each chair. If the dimensions of your space are limited, you can adapt by using fewer chairs and/or shortening the lanes, but the more space you have, the better.

Prepare the ritual by randomly placing tarot cards facedown on the floor of the lanes. Follow your instincts as you choose and place the cards. Be creative. One lane might contain only one card placed at the end, another lane with five cards spaced at equal intervals, and another lane with three cards bunched up in the middle.

Have five readers each take a seat in one of the chairs. Chairs are not assigned; any reader can select any empty chair. Explain that their choices during this fifteen-minute ritual are:

1. Don't move at all.

2. If you do move, stay in your lane.

3. Select cards only from your lane if moved to do so. You can flip the cards over and receive the images immediately or gather the cards to eventually bring back to the chair.

Instruct the participants to allow the tarot cards in their respective lanes to influence them. They may feel energy from one card, just some of the cards, or possibly all of the cards in their individual lanes, or they might not receive any message or connection at all; there is no right or wrong outcome. Encourage them to keep the guidelines in mind, but to stay engaged by listening to shifting rhythms, movements, and thoughts. Initially they might be better served by the powerful choice of complete stillness, and if they decide to leave their chair, slower movements with eyes mostly closed creates a sense of receptivity. Even though it might feel to them like they are performing, encourage them to stay present in their own process.

When everyone understands the guidelines, put on a soundtrack of instrumental music. Ensure quiet from any others in the room. At the end of the exercise, use a bell or simply state "two minutes left" to signal everyone to return to their chairs. When the time is up, the readers are no longer permitted to turn over any cards they have left untouched, or even view cards they may hold in their hands but have not read. If they desire, they are free to look at all of their cards once the group discussion is over. Open the floor for their feedback. Ask how the cards influenced their thoughts and movement. What insights did they gain from this ritual?

The Chairs ritual is a provocative exploration of the nonverbal expression of tarot. Confidence in one's own inner sense of knowing is strengthened by connecting images with internal impulses to move, express the images, or engage the energy with or without looking at the cards.

Tarot Ascension Ritual

Movement surfaces different perspectives. Guided meditation/visualization does as well, especially within a group. It can enhance a sense of connection and heightened energy together. The Tarot Ascension ritual is a group visualization transporting readers into an upper sphere of a tarot world. Provide a deck for those who don't have one.

Have everyone sit in a circle and separate the minor from the major arcana cards in their decks. Have each reader introduce themselves by pulling a card from their minor arcana pile and connecting it to their current energy level. For example, one reader pulls the two of pentacles. They give their name, that they pulled Two of Pentacles, and agree that they have been balancing a lot of things lately. Since they have had a lot on their plate, they are currently feeling tired.

They will keep their chosen minor arcana separate as they shuffle the full deck again. Ask everyone to move to a new place with their cards. As leader, dim the lights and consider using soft drumming to enhance this shift of the ritual.

As the guide, read the following journey using a steady pace. Pause at each * or longer if you observe the need for more time.

"Sit or lie comfortably with your minor arcana check in card. Place the rest of the deck nearby. Take a few minutes to study the card for all of its details. * Close your eyes. Become aware of being in this room. * Our bodies can only be in the present, their greatest gift to us. Let your body and senses bring you fully into this present moment. * There is no past or future. There is only now. * Your breath becomes lower and slower. * A beautiful beam of light comes from above. It is a vibrant color. It connects to the crown of your head. * You feel yourself rise with ease and grace up through this beam.

You float effortlessly as you ascend. * [*soft drumming*] * The light becomes a spiral and swirls about you. It moves slower until it comes to complete stillness. * The spiral dissipates and you find yourself in a live scene of your tarot card. * Look around and see everything in a three-dimensional form of this card. * Who are you in this card? Are you the main person? Are there others in the card with you? How does it feel to be here? * Allow your senses to expand. There is an entire tarot world outside of this scene. The seventy-eight cards are now various places, people, and magical beings of one living world. * Take up your deck. Shuffle and choose cards faceup until you pick a major arcana. * [*soft drumming*] * The major arcana has been expecting your visit. Any minor arcana chosen are on the road to the major arcana. If you received a major arcana right away, imagine traveling straight to them. If not, go through the landscapes of your chosen minor arcana until you see the major arcana's corner of this tarot world. * [*soft drumming*] * As you come close to the major arcana, you feel the electricity of their landscape. * Their environment starts to appear slowly. * You are a welcomed guest. They may or may not appear but you will feel their presence. * For the next few minutes, take your time as you receive a message from this force of nature. * [*drumming*] * Thank this guardian with a gesture. They respond with one as well. * Imagine returning to your original minor arcana scene. You may notice new things along the way. * [*drumming*] *You enter the original scene yet it feels very different now. Notice any outward changes or shifts in your own sense of being here. What is different? * The spiral of light appears. It slowly revolves around you. * You feel weightless as this light around you grows large. * You float down through this beam. * [*drumming*] * The light disappears as your feet touch ground. * Open your eyes and return to your original check in position in the circle."

Feedback can focus on the changes of the minor arcana card from its initial check in to entering and exiting the tarot world. Speaking about the time spent with the major arcana may certainly create a robust dialogue.

The Tarot Ascension ritual produces a strong respect for the minor arcana. It is a metaphorical journey of how the major arcana influences can shift our everyday life. Imagining tarot as a complete world unto itself rather than seventy-eight illustrated cards brings a wholeness as it expands boundaries of reality.

Seer Circle Ritual

Imagining the tarot world is a creative exploration. Another world worth exploring is the ancient past since divination has occurred for centuries. Going deep into our past to surface a world of seers and diviners will also enhance a reader's connection to this art form. The Seer Circle ritual honors those mysterious visionaries through imaginative role play.

Each participant needs a new title for themselves. This title is generated with a selection of a noun and geographical location. I identify myself as a white horse from the Appalachians. For three minutes, have every participant consider their true origins. Encourage everyone to use the Power of Pretend to imagine one's true essence. Allow imagination to soar. Who are you really?

Divide the group in half. One half will shuffle cards and choose one card. These are the seekers, intending to receive a timely insight. The other half are the seers who will take a place around the outskirts of the room. Some may want to strike a pose of a Greek statue or a sphinx.

Each seeker approaches a seer and introduces themselves by their new title. They show their card to the seer, who responds with a brief, truthful insight. Seers can be poetic or speak in riddles if they like, or simply respond with their first thought.

Have everyone return to their original seats. Give the seekers a few moments to record messages. While this happens, each seer shuffles their deck and draws the card they will use when they become a seeker.

Repeat the process with the new set of seekers and seers. When done, the feedback can focus on the experience of being a seer.

The Seer Circle ritual not only pays homage to our historical lineage of divination, it is role-playing at its most sacred. It gives people an opportunity to stretch their ideas of their own identities and abilities to give wisdom.

Summary

A healthy group dynamic requires strong boundaries, clear expectations, and a supportive environment. With these basics in place, rituals from this chapter make up an eclectic menu for four or more participants. These include the use of tarot families, gestures, movement, scanning energy, fictional towns, entering a card, and role-playing as ancient seers.

Chapter Nine

FORMAL RITUALS

Intention is a request to the Creative Unknown. In this chapter, intention takes on the mythic themes of transitions, quests, honoring holy ones and elders, and partnership. Unlike the group rituals of the last chapter, the formal rituals may be enacted with guests and use the Calling the Circle ritual. If one witnesses the ritual but is not part of the sacred circle, suggest that it isn't necessary for them to act or believe in any certain paradigm but they are invited to observe with supportive love.

Of the many rhythms of life, one of the trickiest is transition. Many of us don't handle this shift of energies or circumstances well. Rituals can provide a valuable bridge to acknowledge the need for a pause or integration before the change.

Betwixt and Between Ritual

A versatile ritual, the Betwixt and Between ritual, helps an intimate gathering of students or friends find closure as they end a large group meeting such as a weekend workshop or conference. It is beneficial to set aside some time after the ritual for bonding with food and conversation. Creating sacred space with altars and candles isn't necessary, but is a bonus. An anointing with oils and receiving tarot messages from the group is the highlight of the ritual, but people can elect to refrain from the actual oil blessing.

Have everyone form a circle. Use guidance of the Calling the Circle ritual (pg 17) to open the quarters. Invite everyone to face each quarter as you call the loving guardians of each element with these intentions:

- *East:* Air—"We ask the loving guardians of the east to join us. Bring clarity and insight about this time together and going forward."
- *South:* Fire—"We ask the loving guardians of the south to join us. Help us honor the needs and ideas that surfaced for each of us."
- *West:* Water—"We ask the loving guardians of the west to join us. Help each of us to continue to be a safe haven for all feelings and vision for ourselves and others."
- *North:* Earth—"We ask the loving guardians of the north to join us. Help us hold a deep gratefulness for this time together and share this grace with others."

One by one, each person will move to the center of the circle to be anointed by the person—the blesser—who is standing to their right side in the circle. The blesser uses olive oil or massage oil (or water) as they lightly touch both feet (no need to be barefoot), both palms, the heart center, and the third eye of the person standing in the center of the circle. As each person is being blessed, everyone in the circle pulls one card with the intention of a message for that person's highest potential. Each person will speak to the message of the card with just one sentence. The person in the center closes their eyes through the whole process and receives the anointing and readings.

After all participants have been blessed with oil and messages, poems or self-penned text can be read out loud to consolidate everyone's energy. Close the quarters. Feast or relax with each other afterward.

The Betwixt and Between ritual provides the opportunity to honor every participant with loving touch and tarot messages. The finale of a book, movie, or play has a great influence on how we hold it in our memories. This ritual assures a loving memory.

Quest Ritual

Transitions encapsulate times where risk and uncertainty are necessary. A great change is when someone decides to leave everything that is familiar in their life to get a sense of the life they want to create. For some this might be a road trip, leaving a job, moving to a location of unknowns, or taking a long sabbatical for themselves. The Quest ritual supports this friend, family member, or partner taking a leap of faith. It is a blessing of farewell.

Have the adventurer name who they would want to be present at this farewell ritual. This can be determined by calling on those who are supportive of them. Ask each of the desired guests to create a tarot message beforehand. Have them pull one card (or help them do so if they do not have a deck) and create a message for the adventurer's journey. The intention of the card is to surface a much needed and timely insight. For example, the card chosen is the Six of Cups. The message is, "Six of Cups—We are so proud of you following a dream that you have had in your heart for so long. You are not alone, we are with you in spirit." Have the guest record this advice and seal it in an unmarked, white envelope. Everyone's messages will be given to the adventurer at the time of the ritual.

Using a similar anointing format as the Betwixt and Between ritual, gather in a circle. The traveler will be seated in the center. Everyone will have their sealed envelope. Open the quarters using the intentions:

- *East:* Air—"We ask for the guardians of the east to join us. Send the power of clear thought to bless [*name*] with ease of decision-making and effective use of their communication and powers."

- *South:* Fire—"We ask for the guardians of the south to join us. Send energies of creativity to bless [*name*] to shine brightly as they follow their dream and connect easily to those who are supportive and loving."
- *West:* Water—"We ask for the guardians of the west to join us. Send waves of love to bless [*name*] in creating a true vision and well-being of their life."
- *North:* Earth—"We ask for the guardians of the north to join us. Send your protection to bless [*name*] in all spaces and places."

Announce to the adventurer that they will now be anointed and be given messages of magic for their sojourn. Explain that these messages are to be opened and taken to heart only when called to do so during their journey. Have the adventurer select someone from the circle to anoint them. Invite that person to bless both feet, both palms, the heart center, and the third eye of the adventurer with an oil (or water).

After the anointing, each person of the circle will bring their envelope to the adventurer. Have a bag or basket to collect the envelopes. At this time, every participant can bless them in their own way or say a few words of support. The adventurer is invited to receive the blessings in silence. Close the quarters with gratitude to the guardians.

The Quest ritual expresses the Creative Unknown in tangible ways. The adventurer and their inner circle enter sacred space to invite the guardians to bless this solo journey. The sealed messages will act as synchronistic support for an individual as they travel, move, or take some time for themselves.

Holy One Ritual

Asking for divine support is an act of faith. Divine Allies are mentioned frequently throughout this book because they are forms of the Creative Unknown that we can imagine. The Holy One ritual honors those who help you from the other side of the veil and strengthens your bond and understanding of this unique relationship. Using the Power of Pretend, explore who is on your team. Which guardians support and guide you when needed? How do you relate to source in your everyday life? If you do not have a sense of an invisible ally, you may get a better sense of these divine partnerships by doing the Guide ritual (pg 96).

Determine the Divine Ally, saint, god, goddess, or spiritual energy whom you wish to thank and celebrate. This ritual is particularly effective after a difficult cycle or when requests have been granted. Once selected, research for stories, songs, myths, and history of this beloved helper.

If your ally is personal and only known to you, the Holy One ritual would be done alone. If trusted others have a relationship with your ally as well, the ritual can be done together. For example, my friend and I are both devotees of Saint Barbara, whose feast day is December 4. We work with Saint Barbara's stories as sacred text. Each year we focus on a different aspect. The Holy One ritual honors an ally or guide by celebrating a date that is honored in their name or any time at all.

Create an altar with the holy one's image, symbols, candles, and offerings. Use the Grounding ritual (pg 12) or use the smoke of seasonal herbs. If there are others joining this ritual, wave the smoke over each other. Open the quarters to create sacred space as in Calling the Circle (pg 17). Sit comfortably for a fifteen-minute meditation inviting the holy one to guide your reflections and tarot reading.

After the meditation, discuss or write about your journey and messages received. Allow the experience of the meditation to influence how you will use the tarot. Decide with the others how to create a spread as an effective dialogue with the holy one. After sharing or recording your tarot messages and/or adding to each other's, offer a prayer or poem to express your gratitude for the presence of this blessed being in your life. Close the quarters in gratitude.

To honor a holy one in your life is a powerful and loving gesture of gratitude. Sharing this ritual with others will enhance this connection to them.

Let us now turn to centuries-old rituals acknowledging holy times in one's life. The rites of celebrations and initiations that reflect moon cycles are done in service of the divine feminine: the maiden, the mother, and the crone. The trinity is a powerful symbol of the divine masculine as well. Adapt these rituals accordingly. A non-gendered version of youth, maturity, and elder could be used as an alternative.

Suggested times for each of these three rituals, quarter invocations, activity suggestions, and preparations will be suggested. Guests can be a part of the ritual representing certain aspects, or attend as supportive witnesses. Use Calling the Circle as the structure for the ritual.

Maiden Ritual

Possible Times

- A time that the maiden requests
- Within six months of the first menstruation
- Before the maiden enters middle school
- 11th, 12th, or 13th birthday
- On a new moon

Calling the Circle's Quarter Invocations

- *East:* Incense—Swords suit—"We ask for the guardians of the east to join us. Please give us insights, fresh thoughts, and clear action within the loving powers of the divine feminine."
- *South:* Red candle—Wands suit—"We ask for the guardians of the south to join us. Help us claim our sensuality and sexuality as a vital creative life force."
- *West:* Bowl of water with salt—Cups suit—"We ask for the guardians of the west to join us. Unite us by heart and spirit within the source of all of life and love."
- *North:* Salt or dirt—Pentacles suit—"We ask for the guardians of the north to join us. Give us the wisdom to trust that each of us is an essential part of the circle of life."

Activity Suggestions

- Present and bless a new tarot deck (See Anointing the Deck ritual, pg 23).
- Plant a tree.
- Create a magic bag with each person offering an item such as a crystal or talisman.
- Make a crown of ribbons.
- Anoint the maiden (as in Betwixt and Between ritual, pg 182).

Preparation

- Gather necessary materials for the chosen activity.
- Create beautiful requests or find poems to read at each of the quarters.

- Consider musical needs such as a drum or instrumental music.
- Separate one tarot deck into the four elemental suits, placed at their specific quarters, and position the major arcana in the center.
- Invite four friends to represent and open each quarter.
- Prepare the ritual space using Calling the Circle (pg 17), including an altar with a candle at each of the quarters and in the center.

The Ritual

Using Calling the Circle, open the quarters starting in the east. If there are people representing each quarter, they each will walk slowly around the circle as they bless the space with a representation of their element. For example, the representative of the west may carry their bowl of water and sprinkle water as they walk in the circle. Once they return to their quarter, they invite the guardian by reading the invocation and lighting the candle.

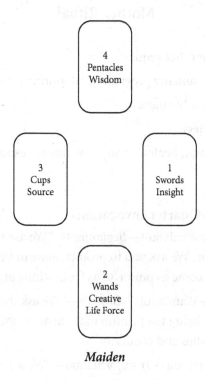

Maiden

The maiden is seated in the center. Invite everyone to sit quietly for five minutes asking the guardians for their blessing of the maiden. After the meditation, the maiden goes to each quarter and selects one card from its elemental suit. They read aloud anything that they sense or think while looking at this card. Others are welcome to share their insights. Designate someone to record the maiden's and guests' insights. For example, the maiden pulls the Knight of Wands at the south quarter altar. In response, the guests speak of great adventures and trust of their sensual nature.

The chosen activity happens after the card selection. Regardless of where you go to engage in the activity, sacred space is in effect until the quarters are closed. Nearing the end of the ritual, have everyone in the circle bless the maiden together with a lovely phrase or by opening their palms to direct loving energy toward the guest of honor. Close the quarters thanking all loving presences. Have fun and food with each other.

Mother Ritual

Possible Times

- A time that the mother requests
- Shortly after announcing pregnancy, adoption, or fostering
- Establishing a new business
- Blessing of a project
- Becoming a mentor, healer, or any new role of responsibility
- On a full moon

Calling the Circle's Quarter Invocations

- *East:* Athame—Swords suit—*Beginnings*—"We ask for the guardians of the east to join us. We ask you to protect *name* in this beginning. Allow clear insights to come as powerful as fresh winds in accepting this call."
- *South:* Incense—Wands suit—*Growth*—"We ask the guardians of the south to join us. Bring the passion that burns brightly to ignite the power of our bodies and creativity."
- *West:* Grail—Cups suit—*Transformation*—"We ask the guardians of the west to join us. Surround us with the depth of love and visions from our muses."

- *North:* Crystals—Pentacles suit—*Manifestation*—"We ask the guardians of the north to join us. Help us remember that as the children of Earth, we are loved and needed."
- *Center:* Seeds—The four aces and the major arcana—*Destiny*

Activity Suggestions

- If pregnant, decorate their belly with a safe henna painting or temporary tattoo markers (the design would be chosen beforehand by the mother and the henna specialist).
- Perform an anointing of the mother (as in Betwixt and Between ritual, pg 182).
- Massage their feet as someone reads a selected story, text, or poem.
- Have each participant make a wish as they tie a knot in a ribbon and weave it into a crown.

Preparation

- Gather necessary materials for the chosen activity.
- Separate the tarot into the cards signified by each quarter.
- Place the four aces and the major arcana at the center altar.
- Invite four friends to represent and open each quarter.
- Consider musical needs such as a drum or instrumental music.
- Prepare the ritual space using Calling the Circle (pg 17) including an altar with a candle at each of the quarters and in the center.

The Ritual

Using Calling the Circle (pg 17), open the quarters starting in the east. Each representative of that quarter will walk slowly around the circle as they bless the space with a representation of their element. Once they return to their quarter, they invite the guardian by reading the invocation and lighting a candle.

Invite everyone to sit quietly for a five-minute meditation asking the guardians for their blessing of the mother. The mother is seated in the center. After the meditation, the mother goes to each quarter and selects one card. The mother reads aloud anything that they sense or think while looking at this card. Others are welcomed to share their insights within the frame of the themes: beginning, growth, transformation, and manifestation of the specific topic being honored. Designate someone to record the mother's and guests' insights. The mother then goes to the center to choose only one ace and one major arcana. The ace as seed and the major arcana as guardian will serve as the focus most needed for the vitality of this journey.

The chosen activity happens after the card selection. Regardless of where you go to engage in the activity, sacred space is in effect until the quarters are closed. Have everyone in the circle bless the mother together. This could be a simple song that someone would lead. Close the quarters thanking all loving presences. Have fun and food with each other.

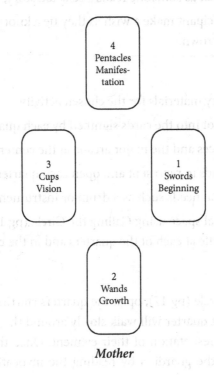

4
Pentacles
Manifes-
tation

3
Cups
Vision

1
Swords
Beginning

2
Wands
Growth

Mother

Crone Ritual

Possible Times
- A time that the crone requests
- Near or over the age of 50

- Having gone through menopause
- Becoming a grandmother
- Retirement

Calling the Circle's Quarter Invocations

A few weeks before the ritual, have the person who will be celebrated as the crone divide the tarot deck into four groups: being, exploring, nurturing, and connecting. Choose only the cards that really speak to these four categories. This selection is made by the crone's intuitive sense alone. Create a discard group for the cards that don't fit well in one of the four groups. The four groups correlate with the four quarters.

- *East:* Toys—Innocence of childhood—*Tarot cards chosen for being*— "We ask for the guardians of the east to join us. Bring us the insights needed to begin the journey of our crone, [name]."
- *South:* Flowers—Energy of the maiden—*Tarot cards chosen for exploring*—"We ask for the guardians of the south to join us. May we open our hearts and bodies to the fires of passion and the creative life force."
- *West:* Spiral or circular object—Love of the mother—*Tarot cards chosen for nurturing*—"We ask for the guardians of the west to join us. Help us flow in the unity of oneness with all mothers human and divine."
- *North:* Salt/dirt and a crown—Wisdom of the elder—*Tarot cards chosen for connecting*—"We ask for the guardians of the north to join us. Accept our crone, [name], into the circle of elders."

Activity Suggestions

- Gather necessary materials for the chosen activity.
- Celebrate the birthday of the new crone by sharing cake and drink.
- Present and bless a book of stories from their friends and family of the influence of their love; read a few excerpts.
- Anoint the crone (as in Betwixt and Between ritual, pg 182).
- Have each participant make a wish as they tie a knot in a ribbon and weave it into a crown.

- Present and bless a new tarot deck (See Anointing the Deck ritual, pg 23).
- Create a magic bag with each person offering an item such as a crystal or talisman.

Preparation

- Place the four groups of tarot cards that the crone has selected at each of the quarters.
- Gather necessary materials for the chosen activity.
- Consider musical needs such as a drum or instrumental music.
- Invite four friends to represent and open each quarter.
- Prepare the ritual space using Calling the Circle (pg 17), including an altar with a candle at each of the quarters and in the center.

The Ritual

Using Calling the Circle, open the quarters starting in the east. Each representative of that quarter will walk slowly around the circle as they bless the space with a representation of their element. For example, the representative of the south may carry flowers as they walk around the circle. Once they return to their quarter, they place the flowers on the altar and invite the guardian by reading the invocation. After the invocation has been read, lighting the candle is always a powerful visual and metaphor.

The crone is seated in the center. Invite everyone to sit quietly for five minutes asking the guardians for their blessing of the crone. After the meditation, the crone goes to each quarter and selects one card. The crone reads aloud anything that they sense or think while looking at this card. Others are welcomed to share their insights within the frame of the themes: childhood, maiden, mother, and becoming crone. Designate someone to record the crone's and guests' insights.

The chosen activity happens after the card selection. The sacred space stays in effect until the quarters are closed. Drum or play instrumental music as everyone sits in silence for five minutes. Have everyone in the circle bless the crone together. Close the quarters thanking all loving presences. Have fun and food with each other.

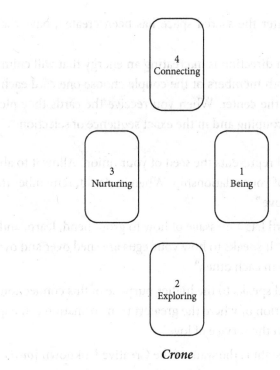

Crone

Ring Blessing Ritual

Another centuries-old ritual is that of marriage. There are two rituals to consider: one is a private affair of blessing the rings and the other is a full wedding based on tarot. The first, the Ring Blessing, is done with the couple before the wedding. Since weddings often include family and friends who may not be comfortable with tarot, this ritual is an intimate and private solution. The ritual's intention is to bless the rings and provide a lifelong reading for the couple.

Meet the couple in a private location within three days of or the day of the wedding. Sunrise is a particularly magical time for this ritual. The wedding rings and your major arcana cards are all that are necessary. Even though you will call the quarters as in the Calling the Circle ritual, no altars, candles, or similar are used. The ritual is barebones, focusing on choosing cards and blessing the rings.

As the leader of the ritual, stand in front of the couple as all three of you face each quarter in turn. Invite the guardians and Beloved Ancestors at each of the directions. After the sacred space has been created, have the couple stand in the center.

The focus of each direction is in creating an energy that will culminate in the ring blessing. Both members of the couple choose one card each for the four directions and the center. When you receive the cards they pick, keep them in their own grouping and in the exact sequence of selection.

- *East:* "This card represents the seed of your union. Allow it to absorb the core value of your relationship. When in doubt, remember this conception of love."

- *South:* "This card has a message of how to grow, bend, learn, and support each other. It speaks to how your egos are shed over and over to surface the best in each other."

- *West:* "This card speaks to the higher purpose of this connection. It shows the direction of where the greatest transformation can happen for yourselves in the service of love."

- *North:* "This insight is the walk of the Creative Unknown [*or the way the couple defines source or spirit*] with your marriage. These are the rewards to be gained and service needed of this union for the world."

- *Center Card:* Each one will pick a card that represents the mystery to unfold over time for each of them. This message is an evolving discovery of their part in this union.

Collect the cards at this time to be interpreted and shared with the couple as a wedding booklet. After the cards have been selected and gathered, it is time for the blessing of the rings. Have each person hold their own ring in their left hand. Direct them to lay their right hand on their partner's cupped hand. Have them close their eyes. Place your hands over both of theirs. Call for the blessings of their guardians and Blessed Ancestors in making these rings sacred. You may want to find or create a prayer or blessing to read at this moment. Signal the closing of this ritual by having the couple join you as you face each quarter to thank and release the guardians. There is magic in this ritual being private and secret. The power will surface at the time of the ring exchange during the wedding.

By the first anniversary of their wedding, create a booklet or document that includes the intentions, all poems or sayings recited, the images of the cards chosen, and a thorough definition of each card. Suggest that they revisit this reading during their wedding anniversaries.

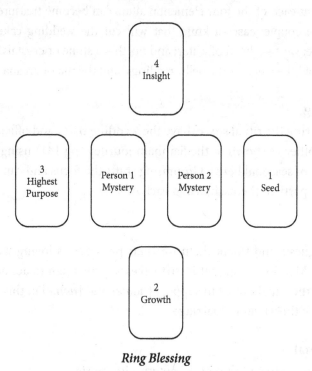

Ring Blessing

Tarot Wedding Ritual

The Tarot Wedding ritual is a full expression of love with tarot as a major aspect. As in the Ring Blessing ritual, the couple selects cards to be interpreted at a later time. Recording each intention, card image, and definition creates a reading that can expand in depth and wisdom over the years for the couple.

The wedding is a true opportunity to provide an energetic net for the couple throughout the length of their marriage. An in-depth conversation with the couple will create a wedding that serves their definition of love and the Creative Unknown. Offer assistance in creating their vows and selecting readings, poems, verses, and songs so that this essence is expressed in all details of the ritual. Consider having the wedding party represent the four quarters. Use Calling the Circle (pg 17) or a variation of it as a basic template. Included is a variation of calling the quarters which invites the four archangels. This ritual works well in an outdoor setting with a great deal of space for the couple and officiant to move about.

Prepare the quarters and center altars with flowers and candles. A sacred tool placed at each of the four elemental altars can become treasured wedding gifts for the couple: east—a knife that will cut the wedding cake; south—a unity candle; west—a bowl of water; and north—a stone or crystals. The center altar will hold the rings, vows, bells, readings, and the major arcana tarot cards.

Grounding

Before entering the ritual space, have the wedding party and officiant ground with each other as shown in the Samhain journey (pg 141) using the smoke of a bundle of seasonal herbs. Grounding shifts the focus and can aid in connecting the party to themselves and each other.

Opening

Greet the guests and thank them for their presence as loving witnesses for the couple. Mention to all that it isn't necessary for them to act or believe in any part of the ritual except to support [name] and [name] in this brand-new beginning of their lives in marriage.

Processional

The wedding party and the couple enters with music.

Calling the Quarters

Invite everyone to stand and face each quarter. Open the quarters with these invocations if using the archangels as the guardians:

- *East:* "I call the mighty Archangel Michael, the Defender, the Prince of Light, to protect us in our hours of need. Fill us with freshness. Let there be clear skies and clear minds to see our way. Let our words create a safe and holy space."
- *South:* "I call the mighty Archangel Uriel, Angel of Repentance. Come gently and let all fear die here within this place. Come into our hearts and warm us. Help us emerge from isolation to greet each other. Let our emotions out from their hiding places."

- *West:* "I call the mighty Archangel Raphael, the Healer, the Guardian of Waters to come and instill us with peace and fulfillment. Help us remember where we came from. Let us all be connected. Let our energies flow smoothly. Let the drought of separation be over."
- *North:* "I call the almighty Archangel Gabriel, the Herald. Send thy wisdom of all sacred beginnings. Strengthen our resolve. Keep us centered. Help us be here now. Let our bodies be strong for loving each other."

Before We Met
Have the couple take positions as far from each other as possible with their backs to each other. As officiant, stay near the center altar and speak:

> *"Go back to the time before you met each other. Think back on who you were then. What did you know about love up to that point? What shape was your heart, mind, and body then?"*

Give them both a few minutes for introspection. Go to each and have them select one card from the deck. Keep the cards separate and place them on the center altar.

When We Met
Instruct the couple to stay in the same position but to turn and face each other and say:

> *"Go to the moment when you first saw each other or recognized each other as your beloved. Recall those feelings and impressions. What do you remember feeling?"*

Give them both some time before having each select one card. Return it to the center altar.

Falling in Love
Direct them to slowly walk toward each other and stop about two feet from one another. As they walk, say:

"Allow yourselves to remember the energy of falling in love
with each other. What trust and courage was needed? Walk in
this magic again. It has led you to this day of commitment."

When you sense it is the right time, go to each and allow them to select one card. Return both cards to center.

Challenge

Have them stay in position but turn their backs to each other.

"Go to those hard times where you had doubt or faced issues
within yourself and with the other. Without judgment,
acknowledge the shadows that may have pulled you away
from love. Send everlasting peace to these struggles."

Have each choose one card.

This Eternal Moment

Direct them to face and move closer to each other. Speak:

"The past and future do not exist. Eternity is all and it is
in this very moment. Be with each other in this sacred
moment. Feel the support of your loving witnesses."

Ask everyone to close their eyes to invite the protection and power of love to embrace *name* and *name*. Ring a bell three times with gracious pauses in between. After the last ring, have each of them choose the final card.

Poems/Verse/ Song

Selections are read or performed by the wedding party.

Vow Exchange

Face one member of the couple and ask:

"Do you [name] *take* [name] *to be your lawfully wedded partner?"*

They respond:

"I do."

"And do you promise to keep them, love and comfort, in sickness and in health, for richer or for poorer, for better or for worse, and to be faithful until death do you part?"

They respond:

"I do."

Repeat with the other partner.

Ring Blessing and Exchange
Face the couple and say:

"May these rings serve as an everlasting symbol of openness and willingness to receive. Surrender is giving up control but not power. Surrender is an act made to increase your own power. When you are willing to receive, you are taking in more love, and when you are taking in more love, you are taking in more independence, more freedom, more source."

As the couple puts the rings on each other's fingers, they say:

"[Name], I give you this ring, in token of my commitment and love."

Poems/Verse/ Song
Selections are read or performed by the wedding party.

Pronouncement
Look at the couple and say:

"By the power invested in me by [state or other governing authority], I now pronounce you spouses for life. You may kiss. We thank the divine ones as witnesses and guides."

Ring the bell before proclaiming:

"This circle is open but never broken."

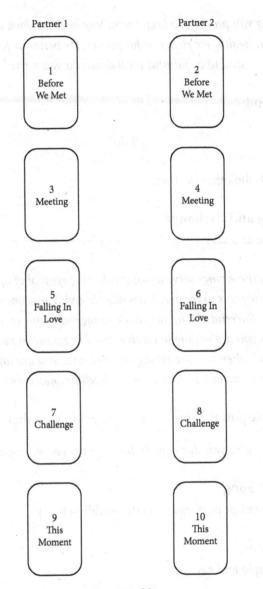

Tarot Wedding

Recessional

The wedding party exits.

On an occasion such as this one, the intent to thank the divine and ringing the bell will sufficiently close the quarters.

By the first anniversary of their wedding, create a booklet or document that includes the intentions, prayers, lyrics of songs used, the images of the cards chosen, and a thorough definition of each card. Suggest that they revisit this reading at every anniversary for ongoing insights.

Summary

The group energy combined within a sacred space produces a powerful intimacy for all involved, whether actively engaged in the ritual or witnessing it. This chapter describes various rituals useful for easing transitions, conjuring support for a person embarking on an adventure, and calling in and offering support to one another's passages in life. The Holy One ritual expresses gratitude for our personal guides and Divine Allies. The three aspects of the divine feminine are given a modern interpretation of centuries-old rituals. The wedding and the blessing of rings are reinterpreted within the wisdom of tarot.

Chapter Ten

CREATING YOUR
OWN RITUALS

This book shares various ways to combine ritual and tarot. You may have already sensed different choices you would make. In this chapter, we discuss how important defining all choices are in creating a ritual that is powerful and effective.

Some key foundational relationships are essential. First, your understanding of the Creative Unknown whether it be a deity, source, love, spirit, our better nature, or other modality determines all else. Doing this work necessitates your own sense of the source of power that you are entering in collaboration with.

Second, your sense of self is key to creating the bridge to the Creative Unknown. How you perceive your own nature as part of this source will be reflected in all aspects of ritual. Identifying either as a spirit having a human experience, an energetic being made of the four elements, a living representation of your ancestors, a white horse from the Appalachians, and/or other realities influences reciprocity with mystery.

A strong personal relationship with the Creative Unknown is essential to avoid misusing energies or wasting your time. As you develop your own understanding, however, do not underestimate the Power of Pretend. Releasing the need for proof and suspending logic allows for new possibilities, much like the Fool as they step off of a cliff into the unknown. Creating the reality you desire and need requires many such leaps of faith.

Tarot rituals make things holy. By trusting your foundation and following your own creative authority, you can create tarot rituals of great magnitude. Pay attention to the impulses or signs that a tarot ritual is needed. These times may include when there is a need to shift energy and power, when you are resisting change, feeling powerless, needing connection, or supporting others' journeys. In a world that has become uncertain for so many of us, follow your passion and curiosity to design the rituals needed by you and others. The following questionnaire gives guidance for creating and personalizing rituals.

Creating a Ritual Questionnaire

The Intention

How was the idea originally conceived?

What needs to be expressed or requested?

What would manifestation of the request look like?

Is this a sacred gathering, an exercise, personal journey, or other?

Structure

Will others be involved in the ritual or will it be solitary?

If others are part of the ritual, what will be expected of them?

Will there be participants that only witness?

Will it be essential to create a strong sacred space by opening the quarters or will simple grounding suffice?

If the ritual is more of an exercise, are you leading?

Tarot Cards

Will the tarot be needed to:

Create the intention?

Act as the major channel for messages during the ritual?

Affirm and clarify the insights gathered during the ritual?

Other?

Activity

What processes are needed to provide an interactive connection with the Creative Unknown:

Reading tarot?

A visualization?

Silent meditation?

Art?

Movement?

Other?

Visuals

What effects would enhance the ritual:

Lighting—candles, moonlight, or sunlight?

Altars for the quarters and/or center?

Flowers or other symbols and objects?

Costumes for the participants?

Other?

Sound

What sounds or music would bring the ritual to another level of experience:

Drumming or instrumental music?

Song?

A bell?

Natural soundscapes such as gently falling rain or waves on a beach?

Planned silence?

Other?

Space

Will this be indoors or outdoors?

What would any movement within the ritual require?

What is needed for a seating arrangement?

How is privacy protected?

Text

What needs to be read or said aloud?

Who needs to speak?

Will poetry or stories provide enhancement?

What invocations will be used if calling the quarters?

Movement

Is there a need to channel energy nonverbally?

Should strong gestures like that of the magician be included?

Should there be basic staging directions, such as walking patterns, for those in the ritual?

Time

Is there a special date, time, or anniversary for this ritual?

How long or short is the ritual?

Are there specific times to be aware of within the ritual, such as a 15-minute meditation?

After you have a basic plan, allow some simmer time for the Creative Unknown to provide additional glimmers or ideas. All healthy relationships, such as the one you are now developing with the Creative Unknown, are reciprocal, so avoid making unilateral decisions.

Return to the six principles (pg 116) to guarantee a healthy flow of the ritual:

- Grounding: Create a neutral space.
- Intent: Allow a true question, request, or desire to surface.
- Form: Choose a structure to gather the insights and clues from the Creative Unknown.
- Synchronicity: Listen and connect to the Creative Unknown's response.
- Closure: Give thanks and say goodbye.
- Integration: Incorporate the magic into your life.

Consider the rituals within this book as basic recipes. As any good cook would do, experiment and add your own taste preferences. Whether by yourself or exploring with a tarot-curious group of friends or students, give your imaginations free rein. Also, whether you are a seasoned tarot reader or not, use your creative authority in determining any messages received through the cards.

Summary

This last chapter brings into focus some things to consider in being the creator of tarot rituals. A questionnaire will help you clarify the need, form, and desired result of any ritual that wants to surface through you. The *Six Principles* are a simple touchstone for rituals whether they are deeply sacred in nature or simple explorations.

CONCLUSION

Tarot rituals are the alchemy of symbolic action and language that together produce a sacred theater. The benefits of investing in your own well-being and creativity are worth the effort and focus this work demands.

Tarot is a blueprint in being divinely human. The minor arcana is a navigation through a world made of elements. The major arcana are portals of love and power. Fully allowing mystery and daily magic builds your creative authority. Always remain true to this. The Power of Pretend will assist you whenever you call on it.

If you are beginning your path of tarot at the time of reading this book, initially put time and focus into the Entering the Card ritual (pg 25). Enjoy and savor this journey into each card because this alphabet will become not only a language but a song.

Earlier I had suggested that you tap the book three times before each opening of it. Some of you who have adhered to this small ritual have your own sense of what this symbolic gesture shifted for you. Others remained loyal to this ritual anticipating an explanation later. My intention for this ritual was to have you knock at your own doors of mystery waiting to be opened. Whether you come to your own conclusion, wait for answers, or have clarity of the mystery, trust that the magic worked.

The Spirit of Tarot is generous and far-reaching. If you don't believe that you are a magical being capable of loving feats, create tarot rituals to show you the road posts. We need your magic.

Blessings on your journey.

SUGGESTED
READING LIST

Antenucci, Nancy, and Melanie Howard. *Psychic Tarot: Using Your Natural Abilities to Read the Cards.* Woodbury, MN: Llewellyn Worldwide, 2011.

Auryn, Mat. *Psychic Witch: A Metaphysical Guide to Meditation, Magick, and Manifestation.* Woodbury, MN: Llewellyn Worldwide, 2020.

Baldwin, Christina, and Ann Linnea. *The Circle Way: A Leader in Every Chair.* San Francisco: Berrett-Koehler Publishers, 2010.

Cehovet, Bonnie. *Tarot, Rituals & You: The Power of Tarot Combined with the Power of Ritual.* Atglen, PA: Schiffer Publishing, 2013.

Cynova, Melissa. *Tarot Elements: Five Readings To Reset Your Life.* Woodbury, MN: Llewellyn Worldwide, 2019.

Elford, Jaymi. *Tarot Inspired Life: Use the Cards to Enhance Your Life.* Woodbury, MN: Llewellyn Worldwide, 2019.

Fairfield, Gail. *Every Day Tarot: A Choice Centered Book.* Boston: Red Wheel/Weiser, 2002.

Foor, Daniel. *Ancestral Medicine: Rituals for Personal and Family Healing.* Rochester, VT: Bear and Company, 2017.

Gordan-Lennox, Jelte. *Crafting Secular Ritual: A Practical Guide.* London: Jessica Kingsley Publishers, 2017.

Graham, Sasha. *Tarot Diva: Ignite Your Intuition Glamourize Your Life Unleash Your Fabulousity!* Woodbury, MN: Llewellyn Worldwide, 2011.

Greer, Mary K. *Tarot for Your Self: A Workbook for the Inward Journey.* Newburyport, MA: Weiser Books, 2019.

Hite, Sheilaa. *101 Tarot Spreads by 20 Tarot Modern Masters*, vol 1. Lenox, MA: The Center for Practical Spirituality, 2016.

McGregor, Andrew. *A Tarot of You: Finding Yourself in the Cards.* Toronto: The Hermit's Lamp Press, 2016.

Moore, Barbara. *Modern Guide to Energy Clearing.* Woodbury, MN: Llewellyn Worldwide, 2018.

Pollack, Rachel. *Rachel Pollack's Tarot Wisdom: Spiritual Teachings and Deeper Meanings.* Woodbury, MN: Llewellyn Worldwide, 2008.

Reed, Theresa. *The Tarot Coloring Book.* Stanford, CT: U.S. Games Systems, Inc., 2016.

Starhawk. *The Earth Path: Grounding Your Spirit in the Rhythms of Nature.* New York: HarperCollins, 2004.

———. *The Spiral Dance: A Rebirth of the Ancient Religion of the Goddess.* New York: HarperCollins, 1979.

Worth, Liz. *The Power of Tarot: To Know Tarot, Read Tarot, and Live Tarot.* Morrisville, NC: Lulu Publishing Services, 2019.

To Write to the Author

If you wish to contact the author or would like more information about this book, please write to the author in care of Llewellyn Worldwide Ltd. and we will forward your request. Both the author and publisher appreciate hearing from you and learning of your enjoyment of this book and how it has helped you. Llewellyn Worldwide Ltd. cannot guarantee that every letter written to the author can be answered, but all will be forwarded. Please write to:

Nancy C. Antenucci
℅ Llewellyn Worldwide
2143 Wooddale Drive
Woodbury, MN 55125-2989

Please enclose a self-addressed stamped envelope for reply,
or $1.00 to cover costs. If outside the U.S.A., enclose
an international postal reply coupon.

Many of Llewellyn's authors have websites with additional information and resources. For more information, please visit our website at http://www.llewellyn.com.